40 DEVOTIONS FOR PRETEEN MINISTRY

BY

CAROL MADER

Group
Groups REAL guarantee

Group LOVELAND, COLORADO

Group's R.E.A.L. Guarantee to you:
Every Group resource incorporates our R.E.A.L. approach to ministry—
a unique philosophy that results in long-term retention and life
transformation. It's ministry that's:

   R E A L

**This is
EARL. He's
R.E.A.L.
mixed up.
(Get it?)**

Relational
Because student-to-
student interaction
enhances learning and
builds Christian
friendships.

Experiential
Because what students
experience sticks with
them up to 9 times
longer than what they
simply hear or read.

Applicable
Because the aim of
Christian education is
to be both hearers and
doers of the Word.

Learner-based
Because students learn
more and retain it
longer when the
process is designed
according to how they
learn best.

Emotion Explosion!
40 Devotions for Preteen Ministry
Copyright © 2000 Carol Mader

Visit our Web site: **www.grouppublishing.com**

Credits
Author: Carol Mader
Acquisitions Editor: Linda A. Anderson
Editors: Jim Hawley and Julie Meiklejohn
Creative Development Editor: Dave Thornton
Chief Creative Officer: Joani Schultz
Copy Editor: Alison Imbriaco
Art Director: Kari K. Monson
Cover Art Director: Jeff A. Storm
Cover Designer: Alan Furst, Inc.
Designer and Computer Graphic Artist: D&G Limited, LLC
Illustrator: Jeff Yesh
Cover Illustrator: Otto Pfannschmidt
Production Manager: Peggy Naylor

Library of Congress Cataloging-in-Publication Data
Mader, Carol.
    Emotion explosion! : 40 devotions for preteen ministry / by Carol Mader.
        p. cm.
    Includes index.
    ISBN 0-7644-2221-9 (alk. paper)
    1. Church work with preteens. 2. Preteens--Prayer-books and devotions--English. 3.
Emotions--Religious aspects--Christianity. I. Title.
    BV4850 .M33 2000
    242'.62--dc21

                                                                                    00-033566

10 9 8 7 6 5 4 3 2   09 08 07 06 05 04 03 02
Printed in the United States of America.

THIS BOOK IS FOR

those counselors who dedicate their lives to helping people look inward, then upward, to move onward, especially Gary L. Thomas, L.P.C., M.A., with my gratitude for the hand that your ministry has had upon mine and the professional resources you shared; Howard Van Culpepper, L.P.C., M. Ed., who answered my questions; and Dr. Amanda W. Ragland, L.M.F.T., C.G.P., and Rev. Jim Norris, L.M.F.T, who presented the Youth Anger Workshop;

my parents, Helen and Larry March, who were there for me; and my brothers and sisters: Catherine March, Steve March, Christine McCurdy, James March, Louise Butler, Patty March, and Tracy Thurston (thank you!);

John Rankin and my friend, Celeste Johnson, with my thanks;

my family at Group, which I'm so proud to be a part of, with special thanks to my editor, Julie Meiklejohn, for her encouragement; Jim Hawley for his work; and Linda Anderson for believing in me.

My deepest gratitude goes to my God for helping me complete this book. "Let them know that it is your hand, that you, O Lord, have done it" (Psalm 109:27).

CONTENTS

INTRODUCTION

Change comes fast and furious to early adolescents and often leaves them and those around them bewildered. The physical changes are obvious. Less apparent—but more volatile—are the emotional issues they face.

Preteens need an opportunity to talk through their feelings. Today's kids are dealing with adult issues at younger ages, and it may be difficult for them to handle all of the complex emotions they feel while continuing to function normally.

Where can kids go with their sorrows and fears, their joys and tears? Through *Emotion Explosion! 40 Devotions for Preteen Ministry*, they will learn from David to cast their cares on the Lord and see how he will sustain them (Psalm 55:22). Using active games, skits, snacks, stories, and art, kids will explore their emotions as they discover a God who affirms and helps them.

In the first chapter of *Emotion Explosion! 40 Devotions for Preteen Ministry*, leaders and kids will discover imaginative ways to recognize and understand their feelings. Through a variety of activities, preteens will explore their emotions and experience creative ways to express them. They will meet David, the author of many of the psalms, who wasn't afraid to feel and express his emotions fully.

The second chapter provides encounters to help participants explore anger, fear, grief, loneliness, distress, and confusion. As preteens learn about guilt, they'll hear the joyful message of forgiveness. When they're tempted to take revenge, preteens will experience waiting upon God. This chapter presents positive, proactive ways to work through negative feelings.

Security, hope, joy, self-worth, and praise are celebrated in the third chapter. Your kids will practice turning their eyes from themselves to the Lord, just as David did. Your preteens will look upward with thanks and praise to our most praiseworthy Lord!

To make this an experience of great meaning and personal exploration, you may want to have each student keep his or her own prayer journal. Throughout the book, you'll find handouts and suggestions for things to include in the prayer journals.

One excellent way to add lasting impact to your group's experience is by developing partnerships with the parents and families. Photocopy the parent letter (p. 81) and send it to your preteens' homes. It provides discussion starters to help families explore their emotions.

May *Emotion Explosion! 40 Devotions for Preteen Ministry*, be a springboard for your students as they plunge into their own hearts and into the beating heart of the Bible—the Psalms!

FEELINGS WE FEEL

Here are some words describing emotions we may feel. First decide if you're exploring positive or negative feelings. Then look under the different headings for words that describe certain emotions. Remember, feelings aren't bad or good—they just are. So have fun exploring your emotions!

HAPPY OR POSITIVE FEELINGS

LOVE

Admired

Appreciated

Comforted

Encouraged

Generous

Genuine

Good

Important

Kind

Liked

Loved

Peaceful

Safe

Sympathetic

Understood

Valued

Worthwhile

JOYFUL

CALM
CHEERFUL
CONTENTED
DELIGHTED
EXCITED
FUNNY
GLAD
GREAT
HAPPY
JOYFUL
POSITIVE
SATISFIED
THANKFUL
WONDERFUL

Powerful

Competent	Energetic
Confident	Hopeful
Courageous	Intelligent
Determined	Secure
	Skillful

UNHAPPY OR NEGATIVE EMOTIONS

SAD

Ashamed
Blue
Burned
Defeated
Degraded
Depressed
Despised
Different
Discouraged

Embarrassed
Excluded
Hopeless
Hurt
Ignored
Insulted
Lonely
Mistreated
Moody
Neglected

Out-of-place
Rejected
Sad
Unhappy
Unloved
Unwanted
Upset
Worthless
Wounded
Victimized

DISTRESSED

Attacked
Awkward
Confused
Disturbed
Doubtful
Helpless
Impatient
Lost
Misunderstood
Offended
Pressured
Stressed Out
Suspicious
Tempted
Trapped
Unpopular
Unsure
Worried

WEAK

Disabled
Empty
Exhausted
Fragile
Helpless
Ignored
Inferior

Insecure
Insulted
Sickly
Uncertain
Unable
Unimportant
Useless

FEARFUL

Afraid
Anxious
Desperate
Hesitant
Insecure
Jealous
Nervous
Overwhelmed
Panicky
Scared
Shy
Tense
Uncomfortable
Worried
Threatened

ANGRY

Aggressive
Annoyed
Cranky
Cruel

Envious
Frustrated
Furious
Hateful
Hostile

Insulted
Intolerant
Irritated
Mad
Vengeful

FOCUSING ON FEELINGS

FEELINGS ARE FRAGILE: HANDLE WITH CARE

Overview: Preteens will learn about respecting each other's feelings as they discover a bottle of fragile "emotions" buried in sand.

Focus Verse: "All my longings lie open before you, O Lord; my sighing is not hidden from you" (Psalm 38:9).

Materials: You'll need Bibles, a small glass bottle or jar with a lid, a bucket or large bowl, rice or sand, small slips of paper, and pens.

Preparation: Write something you're feeling and the reason you're feeling that way on one slip of paper. For example, you might write, "I'm scared because my dad is sick." Put the piece of paper in the bottle, and bury the bottle deep in the sand. Write a more factual statement about yourself on another slip of paper. This statement might describe something you do. For example, you might write, "I play golf on the weekends." Bury the slip of paper in the sand above the bottle. Finally, on a third piece of paper, write a statement about yourself that is public knowledge. For example, you might write, "I have green eyes." Lay that piece of paper on top of the sand.

 ## LIVING PSALM

Ask:

- **What information about yourself do you think God is most concerned with?**
  Pass out Bibles, and have each person look up and read Psalm 38:9. Ask:

- **What do you think this verse means?**

Say: **We human beings are complex creatures made up of layers of skin and layers of feelings. We know that God sees through every layer. But we often show only our outermost layer to the people around us.** Ask a preteen to pick up the first piece of paper and read it aloud. Then say:

Not everyone knows about the things we do. That part is hidden a little deeper. Ask a preteen to uncover and read aloud the next paper. Then say:

Buried in the deepest parts of ourselves are our emotions. We sometimes bury our feelings so well we don't even know they're there. Have another preteen unearth the bottle and read aloud what's written on the paper. Ask:

9

- **Why do you think I might have buried this "emotion" so deep?**

- **Why do you think people conceal their emotions?**

Give each person three slips of paper and a pen, and have everyone write one piece of public knowledge on one of the slips of paper. For example, someone might write, "I am Ashley's brother" or "I have brown hair." Have kids set those slips of paper aside, then have them write one statement about something they do on another slip of paper. For example, someone might write, "I spend a week every summer at my grandma's farm" or "I go fishing with my dad every month." Have preteens set those slips of paper aside. Then have each person write one statement that tells something he or she is feeling and why on the third slip of paper. For example, someone might write, "I feel happy because I'm getting a new puppy" or "I feel scared because my mom and dad have been fighting a lot."

When kids have finished writing, pass around the bottle, and have them put the "feeling" papers in the bottle. Ask one volunteer to bury the bottle in the sand. Then have each person bury the "something I do" statement in the sand above the bottle. Finally, have kids set the public knowledge statements on top of the sand.

LEADER TIP

If preteens don't mention them, you may want to list the following ideas when the bottle returns to you:

- I need to know there's no judgement or criticism.
- I need to know no one will talk about what I say outside this group.
- I need to know no one will laugh at me or make fun of me.

Pass the bucket around, and have each preteen pick up one piece of paper from the top and read the information aloud. Throw away the papers. Then have each preteen dig for and read aloud one of the buried papers. Finally, uncover the bottled emotions and read each of them aloud. Put them back in the bottle, and say:

We often bury our feelings because we're afraid. We're afraid that if people knew how we really felt, they wouldn't like us. People's feelings are fragile, and we need to treat them with respect. I'd like you to think for a moment about what would help you feel comfortable sharing your feelings with this group. For example, maybe you want to know that no one will laugh at you.

Give preteens a few moments to think. Then say: **Now I'm going to pass this bottle of feelings around. When it comes to you, I'd like you to share one thing that you need so that you'll feel comfortable sharing your feelings. God sees and respects our feelings, and we need to do the same for one another.**

POUR OUT YOUR HEART

When you pause during the prayer, have each person say what he or she needs in order to share emotions comfortably.

Dear Lord our God:
You see everything about us, including our feelings. Thank you for being someone we can be completely open and honest with. Help us to respect each other's feelings, Lord. Please help us to (have each person state his or her need). **Thank you for loving us the way we are. Amen.**

FINDING FEELINGS IN THE PSALMS

Overview: Preteens will identify feelings and find those feelings in the Psalms.

Focus Verses: "When can I go and meet with God? These things I remember as I pour out my soul" (Psalm 42:2b, 4a).

Materials: You'll need Bibles; newsprint, tape, and a marker or a dry-erase board and marker; pens; twenty small self-stick notes; and a copy of the "Feelings We Feel" handout (pp. 7-8) for everyone.

Preparation: On the newsprint or dry-erase board, draw two columns. Label one column "Positive" and the other column "Negative."

 ## LIVING PSALM

Say: **Many of the Psalms were written by David, who was king over Israel and Judah. Even though David was a mighty warrior and a powerful king, he was still a man who felt all of the feelings we feel today. David wrote about his feelings in prayers to God and turned them into songs called psalms. His psalms express many emotions, including fear, anger, guilt, and joy. Now we're going to become detectives as we search for clues about how David must have felt as he poured out his soul to God.**

Have the group find the Focus Verses in Psalm 42 and read them aloud together.

• **What do you think the verses mean? When have you felt this way?**

Have the preteens form two teams, the Negatives and the Positives. Give each person a "Feelings We Feel" handout, and give each team a pen and ten self-stick notes.

Say: **I'd like you to look at the handout and, as a team, choose ten emotions. The Negatives will choose negative emotions, and the Positives will choose positive emotions. When your team has agreed on ten emotions, write each emotion on one self-stick note.**

Give teams time to confer and write. Then have preteens stick the self-stick notes to the newsprint or dry-erase board in the appropriate column. Read each note.

Say: **Now I'd like you, in your teams, to search through the Psalms and try to find these emotions. You may not find the exact words for the emotions, so search for the general idea. When you think you've found one of the emotions, either negative or positive, run to the board, take the self-stick note with that emotion written on it, and put the self-stick note in the margin of your Bible next to where you found that emotion.**

> ## LEADER TIP
> Show preteens how some passages may not actually list emotions but may imply them. For example, ask preteens what emotion David is probably feeling when he says, "Come quickly to help me, O Lord my Savior" (Psalm 38:22). Note that we can infer that he felt fear or panic.

Give teams time to search. When all of the self-stick notes have been claimed, have each preteen share a passage the team found and the emotion that passage conveys. Ask:

- **What did you discover about the positive or negative emotions in the Psalms?**

- **What do you think the phrase "I pour out my soul" means? How did you see this demonstrated in the Psalms you looked at?**

- **How do you think David and the other writers of Psalms are similar to you?**

Say: **David and the other writers of Psalms were just as human as we are today, feeling the same emotions we feel.**

 ## Pour out Your Heart

Have preteens join you in prayer by simply sharing some of the passages they found. Ask for volunteers to share. For example, one preteen could pray from Psalm 34:18 "The Lord is close to the brokenhearted and saves those who are crushed in spirit."

Dear Lord:
Thank you for your words expressing so many different types of emotions in the Psalms. (Have volunteers share their chosen psalms.) **Please be with us as we learn more about expressing the way we feel. Amen.**

Ups and Downs With David

Overview: Preteens will "meet" David, learn about some of his major life experiences, and chart the peaks and valleys of his life on poster board.

Focus Verses: "No one whose hope is in you will ever be put to shame" (Psalm 25:3a).

"I have found David son of Jesse a man after my own heart; he will do everything I want him to do" (Acts 13:22b).

Materials: You'll need Bibles, two copies of each page of the "David's Ups and Downs" handout (pp. 15-16), five pieces of white poster board, rulers, pencils, markers, and packing tape.

Preparation: None is needed.

 ## Living Psalm

Say: **Today we'll meet King David, the author of at least seventy-three of the psalms. David's life played out like a thriller movie—an insane king, narrow escapes, fierce giants, and beautiful women were all part of it. As we look at his life, we find David weeping in the dirt and dancing in the streets. We even find him drooling like a madman. David was crowned, cheered, hunted, and jeered. He killed and craved, forgave and prayed. Listen to the Psalms, and you'll hear both David's songs of joy and his mournful wails.**

Through all of his ups and downs, David poured out his heart to his God. That's why we have the Psalms. Let David's words and life transform your own. Like David, you can also be called a person after God's own heart.

Have kids form four teams, and assign each team a number from one to four. Ask teams to choose a team member for each of these roles: Reader, Artist, Writer, and Director. Give each team

Bibles, a piece of poster board, a "David's Ups and Downs" handout, a ruler, a pencil, and markers.

Begin by having the Readers look up and read aloud the Focus Verses, Psalm 25:3a and Acts 13:22b. Then say: **Next, I'd like the Readers to read from the handout the events describing the part of David's life assigned to your teams. The rest of the team will need to listen carefully and determine where David's ups and downs occurred.**

When the Readers are finished, the Artists will take over. You'll need to measure the poster board and mark the halfway point from top to bottom. (Use the extra piece of poster board to demonstrate what the Artists are to do.) **Then draw a faint pencil line across the middle of the poster board; you'll be erasing the line later. When you've done this, the rest of the team can tell you how to chart David's ups and downs. Begin at the far left side of your line, then draw a line either up or down, according to the experience David had. Continue in this way until you've reached the end of your poster board and you've charted all of the experiences your team was assigned.**

When the Artists are finished, the Writers will take over. Writers, you'll need to write a brief description of what happened during each of David's ups and downs. Try to limit each description to one sentence. For example, an "up" might be "David killed Goliath." Writers, when you're finished with that, you'll need to write your team's portions of the Focus Verses on the top and bottom of your poster board. You'll find the verses on your handout. Throughout this experience, the Directors need to be encouraging each team member to complete his or her task. **If team members have time after these tasks are completed, they can use the markers to draw pictures or symbols of David's experiences.**

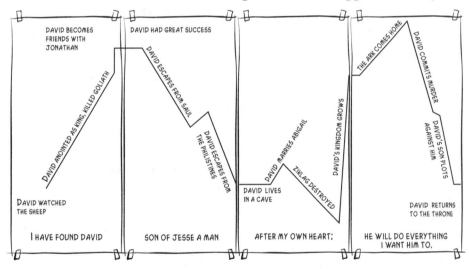

Give teams time to work on the posters. When all the teams are finished, use the packing tape to attach their posters together, numbered in order from left to right, and hang them on a wall. Have the Director from each team read the team's chart aloud to the group.

Ask:

- **What feelings do you think David felt during some of these experiences?**

- **Why do you think God allowed David to go through his bitter experiences?**

- **Why do you think David was called a man after God's own heart?**

- **What does it mean to have a heart after God's own? How could you have a heart like that?**

POUR OUT YOUR HEART

Have preteens bow their heads as you pray this prayer aloud.

Dear Lord:

Thank you for every hard time and every happy time in David's life. We see that David looked to you, whether he faced happy or hard times. As we go through the ups and downs in our own lives, please make us into people after your own heart. Amen.

> **• EXTRA IMPACT •**
>
> Have preteens map the major experiences in their own lives. First they can chronicle their histories in a list format and then make charts on paper. Have each preteen turn his or her chart into a prayer by writing across the top of the chart, **"Lord, thank you for being with me through my ups and downs** (list ups and downs). **Give me a heart like yours."** Have kids put these charts into their journal notebooks.

THE SHADES OF FEELINGS

Overview: Preteens will hear David's feelings expressed, identify the feelings with colors, and paint a collage.

Focus Verses: "For you make me glad by your deeds, O Lord; I sing for joy at the works of your hands. How great are your works, O Lord, how profound your thoughts!" (Psalm 92:4-5)

Materials: You'll need Bibles, newsprint, poster paints in various colors, cups of water, paintbrushes, foam plates, copies of the "Feelings We Feel" handout (pp. 7-8), and pens.

Preparation: Set out the paint, one color per foam plate, and cups of water.

LIVING PSALM

Begin by reading the Focus Verses, Psalm 92:4-5 aloud. Say:

You may have heard someone talk about being blue. Blue is a color sometimes used to describe feeling down. Different feelings might be described with different colors. Today we're going to choose colors to portray feelings and paint the colors into a mural as psalms are read.

Give each preteen a paintbrush. Say: **I'm going to read aloud several passages from the Psalms. As I read, I'd like you to choose the color you think represents the feelings you hear expressed in each passage. Then paint brush strokes of that color on the newsprint.**

Choose some or all of the following passages to read aloud: Psalms 25:15-17; 26:8; 28:7; 30:1-3; 39:2-5; 40:1-2; and 51:1-4. (You may want to ask for volunteers to read one passage each.)

When preteens have finished painting, distribute "Feelings We Feel" handouts and pens, and have preteens choose feelings to label the colors. Encourage them to use a variety of feeling words that are not as familiar to them. For example, the shades of anger may go from annoyed all the way to vengeful. When all the colors have been labeled, ask:

DAVID'S UPS AND DOWNS

TEAM ONE

- David lived in Bethlehem. He came from a family of eight boys. His job was to tend the sheep. While he was in the fields, he learned to play the harp. David also learned to trust God when a lion or bear prowled nearby (1 Samuel 16, 17).

- When David was still young, God chose him as the next king. God sent Samuel the priest to Bethlehem. David was in the field when Samuel arrived, and no one told him to come home to meet Samuel. Samuel sent for David. He poured oil on David's head as a sign that he would one day be the king (1 Samuel 16).

- A nine-foot giant named Goliath was harassing the army of Israel. Not one soldier would fight him. But David fought him, saying, "The battle is the Lord's!" He killed the giant with one stone. After that, David's life would never be the same (1 Samuel 17).

- King Saul had a son named Jonathan who became David's very best friend. They both had big hearts, an unshakable faith in God, and a love for adventure. Jonathan saved David's life even though Jonathan could have been the next king (1 Samuel 14, 19).

- Write on the top of your poster board this segment of Psalm 25:3a: "No one."

- Write on the bottom of your poster board this segment of Acts 13:22b: "I have found David."

- -

TEAM TWO

- In everything he did, David had great success because the Lord was with him. David became a famous warrior. King Saul grew jealous of all the attention David got. While David was playing the harp for him, Saul hurled his spear at him but missed (1 Samuel 18, 19).

- David's wife, Michal, helped David escape from King Saul, her crazy father. After David climbed out a window, Michal put a statue in David's bed to deceive Saul's soldiers. The trick worked, and David fled to Samuel, the high priest. David became a hunted man (1 Samuel 19).

- Three times, Saul sent soldiers to get David. But, instead of capturing David, the soldiers were captured by God, and they prophesied with Samuel's people. Then Saul went himself, but he did the same thing. David must have laughed as he ran away (1 Samuel 19).

- David escaped to the Philistines. Some of the Philistines realized David was the one who had killed their Goliath; they tried to grab him. But David pretended to be a crazy person, drooling and acting wild. The king told him to get out. He ran to hide in a cave (1 Samuel 21).

- Write on the top of your poster board this segment of Psalm 25:3a: "whose hope is in you."

- Write on the bottom of your poster board this segment of Acts 13:22b: "son of Jesse a man."

DAVID'S UPS AND DOWNS

TEAM THREE

- David hid in the wilderness, and men came to join him. Soon he had an army of six hundred men. One day, while David and his men were in a cave, King Saul came into the care. David could have killed him easily, but he didn't. Saul said he was sorry for hunting for David and that he would leave David alone. But Saul never did (1 Samuel 24).

- David became very angry with a fool named Nabal and was about to attack Nabal's household. Nabal's wife, Abigail, went to meet David with gifts for him. She begged him to not take revenge. David listened. Soon after that, Nabal died, and Abigail became David's new wife (1 Samuel 25).

- David went back to live in the land of the Philistines. When the Philistines went to war against Israel, enemies attacked David's city, Ziklag. Then David's men turned against him. He thought he had lost everything. But David trusted in God. And God came through (1 Samuel 27-30).

- Within twenty-four hours, David got everything back. Saul died, so David was now ready to become the king. David's kingdom grew stronger as his army won wars. David won the hearts of the people, and he pointed them to God. God blessed David (1 Samuel 30, 2 Samuel 1-3, 5).

- Write on the top of your poster board this segment of Psalm 25:3a: "will ever be."

- Write on the bottom of your poster board this segment of Acts 13:22b: "after my own heart."

TEAM FOUR

- David brought the Ark of God home to Jerusalem. There was a big celebration. David was so happy that he leaped and danced before the Lord. God promised David that his kingdom would last forever. Jesus is a descendant of David's family line (2 Samuel 6-7).

- David had many victories. But everyone remembers this huge mistake: David took another man's wife as his own. Then he made sure that her husband would be killed in a war. God was angry with David. David was sorry for his sin, and God forgave him (2 Samuel 11-12).

- David had many wives and children. His son Absalom decided he wanted to be the king instead of David. He turned many people away from David. When David heard about this, he and the people in his palace ran away to save their lives (2 Samuel 15).

- While David was hiding in the desert, Absalom came after him. But Absalom's hair got caught in a tree, and he was killed. David was able to return to the throne. His son Solomon became the next king when David died. What a life David lived! (2 Samuel 18, 1 Kings 1).

- Write on the top of your poster board, Psalm 25:3a: "put to shame" (Psalm 25:3a).

- Write on the bottom of your poster board, "he will do everything I want him to do." (Acts 13:22b).

- **Why did you choose to match these colors with these emotions?**

- **What feelings did you hear David express that surprised you?**

- **Why is it important to be able to identify feelings?**

Ask volunteers to point to feeling labels and share times they experienced those emotions.

 ## POUR OUT YOUR HEART

Ask each person to choose one of the colors labeled with an emotion. As you pray, pause after you list each color, and let preteens name the emotions they associate with the color.

• EXTRA IMPACT •

The Psalms were written as songs of praise to God. Over the years, the music has been lost. Some artists have turned them back into songs. While the colors are being painted, play some recorded versions of the Psalms. One good choice is "Psalms: Music to Soothe the Soul" (Essential Records). The music learners in your class, especially, will benefit from musical interpretations of the Psalms. You may even want to invite someone in to play interpretive guitar music as the Psalms are read.

Dear Lord Our God:
Thank you for the times we feel (list the colors on the mural. Pause after each to allow preteens to share the emotions they associate with the colors.) **You are a God of feeling. Thank you for giving us feelings. Help us share all our feelings with you, as David did. Amen.**

SENSING GOD'S GOODNESS

Overview: Create a banquet of food and draw pictures to celebrate the goodness of God.

Focus Verse: "Taste and see that the Lord is good" (Psalm 34:8a).

Materials: You'll need Bibles, poster board, markers, a CD or cassette of praise music, a CD or cassette player, the various food items kids bring to the devotion (see Preparation), and utensils to serve and eat them.

• EXTRA IMPACT •

Instead of having food brought to the devotional, plan a special trip to the market. Contact kids in advance so they'll have money to buy food. Have kids form teams, and have teams choose one or two items. If the weather is nice, you could do this devotional as a picnic on or off the church grounds. Be sure to take the necessary precautions if you take kids off church grounds.

Preparation: A few days before you use this devotion, contact kids, and ask them to bring a favorite food with them to this meeting. Encourage kids to bring something they'd enjoy giving to someone else. You'll also need to set up a table (or tables) for the food.

 ## LIVING PSALM

Have kids place the food they brought on the table. Say: **In one of his psalms, David used his senses of taste and sight to describe God. The Focus Verse for today, Psalm 34:8a, says, "Taste and see that the Lord is good." First, let's use these food items we brought to taste the Lord's goodness.**

Have kids gather around the table of food. Say: **Think about how the food item you brought could represent God's goodness. For example, if you brought a cola, you could say the energy you get from drinking the cola is like the energy your faith gives you.**

Have each person describe the food he or she brought and say why it represents God's goodness. Allow time to enjoy the food.

Then have kids form groups of three or four, and provide one sheet of poster board and markers for each group. Say: **David's psalm also says to "see that the Lord is good." I'd like each of you to draw something that helps you see God's goodness. For example, you might draw a stream and say, "I feel peaceful when I see this stream."**

Play the praise music while the kids work on their posters. When they're finished, ask:

- **How did your sense of taste or sight help you see God's goodness?**

- **What do you think David meant when he said, "Taste and see that the Lord is good"?**

- **How could you use your other senses to celebrate God's goodness?**

 ## POUR OUT YOUR HEART

Have each group show its poster, and ask kids to take turns describing how the picture helps them see God.

Dear Lord:
Thank you for the senses you have given us. We praise you because of your goodness. We taste and see that you are good! Amen.

CARTOON CAPERS

Overview: Preteens will cut out cartoon faces and match them to feeling words as they practice using "I feel" statements.

Focus Verse: "Search me, O God, and know my heart" (Psalm 139:23a).

Materials: You'll need Bibles, pages of newspaper comic strips, scissors, glue sticks, construction paper, pens, and copies of the "Feelings We Feel" handout (pp. 7-8) and the "911—Psalms to the Rescue!" handout (pp. 21-22). (Note: the "911—Psalms to the Rescue!" handout is also used in the Disaster 911 devotion in Chapter 2.)

Preparation: None is needed.

LIVING PSALM

Ask: **What is your favorite comic strip or cartoon? Tell me about it.**

Allow kids to share examples. Then say: **Cartoon characters express a wide variety of emotions. And the words in the Psalms express many emotions as well. Today we're going to identify and express some feelings using comic strip characters and some of the Psalms.**

Have preteens form pairs, and give each pair a "911—Psalms to the Rescue!" handout, a page of comic strips, a piece of construction paper, scissors, a glue stick, and a pen. Have each pair search the comic strips for faces that show a variety of emotions. Have kids cut out the faces and glue them onto the construction paper, leaving space between the faces to write in. Ask each pair to fill the paper with faces that express a range of feelings, such as joy, distress, and anger.

Then ask pairs to draw a speech bubble coming from each character's mouth and write what the character might be saying about his or her feelings in the bubble. The words in the speech bubble should begin with "I feel," followed by a description of the feeling that includes at least two similar words. For example, if a pair finds a picture of Sarge ringing Beetle Bailey's neck, the preteens might write, "I feel aggravated, exasperated, and irritated!"

When preteens have finished a speech bubble for each character, have them draw a second speech bubble for each character next to the first one. In the second bubble, have pairs record some of David's words expressing the same sentiment. Encourage pairs to use the "911—Psalms to the Rescue!" handout to help locate appropriate passages. If they prefer, they can search Psalms themselves. For the above example, a pair might write, "Do not grant the wicked their desires, O Lord" (Psalm 140:8a) in the bubble next to Sarge's "I feel" bubble.

When a pair is finished with its sheet, have one person write the Focus Verse, Psalm 139:23a, across the top. Then have kids pass their papers around for everyone to enjoy.

LEADER TIP
You may want to go to the office of your local newspaper to get back copies of older comic strips to provide variety, especially if your class is large.

Ask:

- **What were some words you saw that describe anger? fear? joy?**

- **Why is it important to know how to identify your feelings?**

- **Turn to your partner and answer this question: Which one of the cartoon characters on your sheet expresses how you felt at one time this week? What situation occurred to make you feel like that?**

Say: **God searches us and knows our hearts, even the feelings that we don't share with anyone. Let's ask him to help us know our own emotions.**

 POUR OUT YOUR HEART

Have students bow their heads as you pray this prayer aloud.

Dear Lord our God:
Thank you for the fun we can have talking about feelings and sharing our feel-
ings. Thank you for giving people talent to make cartoons to make us smile.
Please help us learn to identify our feelings and then express them to you. Search
us, O God, and know our hearts. Help us to know them too. Amen.

ART SMART

Overview: Preteens will discover that drawing is a unique way to express their feelings.

Focus Verse: "I am a worm and not a man, scorned by men and despised by the people" (Psalm 22:6).

Materials: You'll need Bibles; newsprint, tape, and a marker or a dry-erase board and marker; paper; pencils; and copies of the "Feelings We Feel" handout (pp. 7-8).

Preparation: None is needed.

 LIVING PSALM

Say: **David expressed his emotions on paper by writing beautiful songs. He painted detailed pictures with words just as an artist uses colors on a canvas. As we read Psalm 23, we can close our eyes and hear the music of a gentle brook flowing over rocks. In Psalm 40, we see a man getting pulled from muddy quicksand to stand victoriously on a rock. Picture a tornado breaking great branches from the trees as we read Psalm 29.**

> **• EXTRA IMPACT •**
> Let your students find more passages that seem visually alive. You might suggest they check out these Psalms for animated descriptions: Psalm 22; 98; 102; 104; 114; 116; 126; 133; 144; and 147.

Some people express themselves best by drawing. We're going to read a story in the life of David and draw a picture to illustrate how he might have felt.

Give each person a Bible. Have the students open their Bibles to 1 Samuel 30:1-6 and follow along as you read the story aloud. Then ask:

• David's home was burned, the women and children were captured, and David's men were talking about stoning him. How do you think David felt?

• How would you draw the way David felt?

Ask for a volunteer artist. Read Psalm 22:6 aloud, and ask the artist to illustrate this verse on newsprint or a dry-erase board for the group to see. The volunteer can think of his or her own drawing or copy the worm drawing in the margin. Have another volunteer write a prayer on the drawing. For example, the

911—Psalms to the Rescue!

Turn to these psalms for comfort when you feel:

Angry

- "But when I was silent and still, not even saying anything good, my anguish increased. My heart grew hot within me" (Psalm 39:2-3a).
- "Break the teeth in their mouths, O God; tear out, O Lord, the fangs of the lions!" (Psalm 58:6).

Vengeful

- "Repay them for their deeds and for their evil work; repay them for what their hands have done and bring back upon them what they deserve" (Psalm 28:4).
- "Awake, and rise to my defense! Contend for me, my God and Lord. Vindicate me...do not let them...say 'We have swallowed him up' " (Psalm 35:23-25).
- "O Lord, the God who avenges, O God who avenges, shine forth. Rise up, O Judge of the earth" (Psalm 94:1-2a).

Confused

- "Show me your ways, O Lord, teach me your paths; guide me in your truth and teach me, for you are God my Savior, and my hope is in you all day long" (Psalm 25:4-5).
- "Your word is a lamp to my feet and a light to my path" (Psalm 119:105).
- "The unfolding of your words gives light; it gives understanding to the simple" (Psalm 119:130).

Guilty

- "I said, 'I will confess my transgressions to the Lord'—and you forgave the guilt of my sin" (Psalm 32:5b).
- "If I had cherished sin in my heart, the Lord would not have listened" (Psalm 66:18).
- "Search me, O God, and know my heart" (Psalm 139:23a).

Lonely

- "I am a worm and not a man, scorned by men and despised by the people" (Psalm 22:6).
- "Even my close friend, whom I trusted, he who shared my bread, has lifted up his heel against me" (Psalm 41:9).
- "Listen to my cry, for I am in desperate need" (Psalm 142:6).

FEARFUL

- "Do not be far from me, for trouble is near and there is no one to help." (Psalm 22:11).
- "My heart has turned to wax; it has melted away within me" (Psalm 22:14b).

DISTRESSED

- "Hear me, O God, as I voice my complaint. Protect my life from the threat of the enemy" (Psalm 64:1).
- "But you, O Lord, sit enthroned forever...He will respond to the prayer of the destitute" (Psalm 102:12a, 17a).
- "Then they cried out to the Lord in their trouble, and he delivered them from their distress" (Psalm 107:6).

SAD

- "All my longings lie open before you, O Lord; my sighing is not hidden from you" (Psalm 38:9).
- "The Lord has heard my weeping...The Lord accepts my prayer" (Psalm 6:8b, 9b).
- "How long must I wrestle with my thoughts and every day have sorrow in my heart?" (Psalm 13:2a).

SECURE

- "I have set the Lord always before me. Because he is at my right hand, I will not be shaken" (Psalm 16:8).
- "I will instruct you and teach you in the way you should go; I will counsel you and watch over you" (Psalm 32:8).
- "Surely God is my help; the Lord is the one who sustains me" (Psalm 54:4).
- "By this I will know that God is for me" (Psalm 56:9b).

JOYFUL

- "You, O Lord, keep my lamp burning; my God turns my darkness into light" (Psalm 18:28).
- "My heart leaps for joy and I will give thanks to him in song" (Psalm 28:7b).
- "For you make me glad by your deeds, O Lord; I sing for joy at the work of your hands. How great are your works, O Lord, how profound your thoughts!" (Psalm 92:4-5).

THANKFUL

- "My heart may sing to you and not be silent. O Lord my God, I will give you thanks forever" (Psalm 30:12).
- "I will give you thanks in the great assembly; among throngs of people I will praise you" (Psalm 35:18).
- "You are my God, and I will give you thanks" (Psalm 118:28a).

volunteer might write, "Lord, I feel rejected, hated, and alone. Please help me. I know you'll never leave me. Amen."

Give each person a "Feelings We Feel" handout, a piece of paper, and a pencil, and say: **Now it's your turn. Draw your own picture prayer. Use the "Feelings We Feel" sheet to find words to describe your own feelings. Then draw a picture to express the feeling, and write a prayer near the picture. For example, you might draw a picture of yourself holding onto a tree limb with a written prayer under it that says "Lord, I am exhausted. I am about to fall. Please help me to hold on!" Or you might draw yourself on a hang glider and write in the clouds, "Lord, I feel so relieved I could fly. Thank you for forgiving me!"**

> **• EXTRA IMPACT •**
> Allow your artistic kids an opportunity to express themselves. Hang newsprint and let them draw a class mural full of images. Someone might draw waves lifting high with the words, "The seas have lifted up their pounding waves" (Psalm 93:3b). Another person might illustrate Psalm 18 to show the Lord parting the heavens and mounting the angels to soar "on the wings of the wind." Leave the mural up for the kids to add to as they discover more imagery.

Give preteens several minutes to draw their prayers.

Pour out Your Heart

Ask if any of the kids are willing to share their picture prayers aloud with the group. Close by praying the following prayer together.

Dear Lord:
There have been times in my life when I've felt like a worm, alone and rejected by other people. It feels awful and scary. David found strength in you when he felt like that. Please help us always to come to you with our needs. Thank you for never rejecting us. Amen.

Body Language Talks

Overview: Preteens will use pantomime to express David's stories and feelings through body language.

Focus Verses: "Clap your hands, all you nations; shout to God with cries of joy" (Psalm 47:1).

"David...danced before the Lord with all his might" (2 Samuel 6:14).

Materials: You'll need Bibles and copies of "Body Language" (p. 24).

Preparation: None is needed.

Living Psalm

Say: **One study showed that the verbal part of our messages accounts for only seven percent of what is communicated. Tone of voice accounts for thirty-eight percent, and our nonverbal communication accounts for a whopping fifty-five percent of the message that comes through. In other words, our bodies can "shout" quite silently.**

David didn't let his anger grow inside him. He expressed his feelings, and we can learn to do the same. Today we're going to explore together some examples from David's life and express them using our body language.

Give each person a Bible. Have preteens form groups of four, and give each group a copy of "Body Language." (If your group is large, have two groups do a story-psalm combination.) Assign each group one of the following story and psalm combinations:

- **Story of Fear:** Saul sends men to David's home. (1 Samuel 19:11-17; Psalm 59:1-5, 16-17)

- **Story of Sadness and Fear:** David acts like a madman. (1 Samuel 21:10-15; Psalm 34:17-22)

- **Story of Anger:** Doeg murders the priests. (1 Samuel 22:6-23; Psalm 52)

- **Story of Joy:** The ark comes home. (2 Samuel 6:16-21; Psalm 30)

Say: **You'll be presenting skits to share what your stories and psalms are about. First, I'd like each group to read through your assigned Scriptures together.**

When groups are finished reading, say: **Each group should have two Readers, one Actor, and one Director. One Reader will put David's story into his or her own words, and the other Reader will choose verses from the psalm to add to the story as they fit. As the Readers share the story from David's life and David's feelings as he expressed them in the psalm, the Actor will pantomime the action in the story. He or she will probably need to play several roles. The Director will oversee the action and offer suggestions. Use the ideas in the "Body Language" box to help express the emotions the characters were feeling.**

Have groups practice their pantomimes and then present them to the entire group.

After the performances, ask:

- **Why wasn't David embarrassed to express his feelings?**

- **Why are we so often afraid to express our feelings?**

- **What types of feelings do you wish you felt more free to express? Explain.**

Read aloud the Focus Verses, 2 Samuel 6:14 and Psalm 47:1. Say: **The Psalms encourage us to express our feelings and clap our hands and shout to God.**

BODY LANGUAGE

Use exaggerated movements and facial expressions.

Fear

Wide-open eyes, hands over face, standing frozen in place, darting glances, jerky or stiff movements, shaking hands, quick and shallow breathing, held breath, chattering teeth, sweating

Sadness or Grief

Frowning expression, eyes watering, body shaking with sobs, head down or in hands

Anger

Scowling expression, furrowed brow, tight fists, red face, hands on hips, body leaning forward, tensed body

Joy

Smiling expression, laughter, hands held up in the air, bouncy movements

POUR OUT YOUR HEART

At the appropriate time in the prayer, pause to allow kids to silently express themselves using body language. After praying this prayer together, have kids clap their hands for God.

Dear Lord:
Thank you for allowing us to express our feelings. Help us to be honest with you about our feelings. Please see our body language as our prayer Pause. **We love you. Amen.**

• EXTRA IMPACT •
For more fun with body language, show preteens a movie clip with the sound turned off. Ask them to list as many feeling words as they can as they see them. After the clip, ask kids to compare their lists.

FEELINGS HELD HOSTAGE

Overview: Preteens will share in an object lesson about escalating inner conflict that ultimately explodes.

Focus Verse: "But when I was silent and still, not even saying anything good, my anguish increased. My heart grew hot within me, and as I meditated, the fire burned" (Psalm 39:2-3a).

Materials: You'll need Bibles; an empty eight-ounce plastic container with a lid, such as a plastic yogurt container; effervescent antacid tablets; a pitcher of water; poster board; scissors; a marker; glue; newspaper.

Preparation: Try this object lesson at home first so you'll know the correct ratio of tablets and water to use.

Cut a circle of poster board a little bigger than the container's lid. Draw an expressionless face on the circle, using just a line for the mouth. Around the features, write, "I'm not _____. This is not a problem for me. This is not affecting me. If I ignore this feeling, it will go away." Glue the poster-board circle on the lid.

LIVING PSALM

Set the container on old newspaper on the floor. Have preteens gather around the container and say: **God created our feelings so we could do something with them. He gave us anger so we could channel it to change what's wrong. He gives us warm feelings for people so we can hug them. He gives us feelings of fear so we can avoid bad**

• EXTRA IMPACT •

Give each person an empty 35-millimeter film container and half an antacid tablet. Have each person share a feeling with a partner and then add a few drops of water to the container. After the containers explode, have pairs talk about ways to let that feeling out without hurting anyone or themselves.

Note: This activity would work best in a gym or outdoors. The containers themselves can be dangerous when they "explode." Try the exercise yourself first so you know what kind of force is involved.

---

situations. But too often, we take our feelings and bury them inside ourselves. Feelings locked inside us can become dangerous.

Fill the container nearly full of water. Give each person an antacid tablet, and ask each person to share a feeling that's easy to bury inside. Then have students quickly "plop" the tablets into the water, and put the lid on.

Say: **Ignoring feelings won't make them disappear. They simmer inside us like water in a pot about to boil.** Read aloud the Focus Verse, Psalm 39:2-3a. **If we ignore, deny, or lie about our feelings, they stay locked inside of us until we...pop!** After the container has blown its top, ask:

- **What happened to this "person" when his feelings were held in?**

- **What happens to real people when they hold their feelings in? What do they do?**

- **What types of feelings can build up inside of people?**

- **How can you get your feelings out in good ways so that you don't "pop"?**

Say: **We all know people who lose their tempers because they're not handling their anger well. But it's not just unhappy feelings that we keep inside. We may love someone and want to tell that person, but we don't. Sometimes we are proud of ourselves, but we're afraid to brag. Now I'd like each of you to choose a partner and share one feeling that you have kept inside or that you have the tendency to keep inside. Then discuss how you can share those feelings in positive ways.**

 ## POUR OUT YOUR HEART

Have kids bow their heads as you pray this prayer aloud.

Dear Lord:
Thank you for making us people full of feelings. Please teach us how we can handle our feelings in good ways. Help us to share our true feelings with you and others, just as David did. Amen.

DRIBBLE-DRABBLE PRAYERS

Overview: Preteens will use an eyedropper and a cup to see the difference between shallow prayer requests and heartfelt prayers to God.

Focus Verse: "Trust in him at all times, O people; pour out your hearts to him, for God is our refuge" (Psalm 62:8).

Materials: You'll need Bibles, slips of paper, pen, two eyedroppers, two cups, three buckets, and water.

Preparation: Write these references on slips of paper so that you have two slips of paper for each reference: Psalm 13:1-2; 17:1; 18:6; 21:1; 22:11-14; 27:7; 30:11-12; 31:6-7; 31:9-10; 34:1-4; 42:1-4; or 95:1-2. Use the slips of paper to mark the passages in two Bibles.

 LIVING PSALM

Have the preteens form two teams, and have the teams stand next to each other at one end of the room. Put a bucket filled with water between the two teams. Set up two chairs at the opposite side of the room, one chair opposite each team. Place one of the Bibles you prepared on each chair, and put an empty bucket next to each chair. Give each team an eyedropper and a cup.

Say: **Sometimes our prayers are "dribble-drabble" prayers. Dribble-drabble prayers don't involve much thought or feeling. For example, when you say prayers you've memorized, you might say them without thinking about what you're saying. But God wants to know the real you. He wants to know your honest feelings and thoughts.**

Fill an eyedropper with water and squeeze it into one of the buckets as you say a few memorized prayers or simplistic requests, such as, "Bless Grandma," "Bless me," or "Please give me a new video game." Then open your Bible to Psalm 102:1 (or another similar passage) and fill a cup with water. As you read Psalm 102:1, pour the cup of water into the bucket.

Have team members take turns filling an eyedropper with water, walking across the room, and praying a dribble-drabble prayer as they squeeze the water into the bucket. Then have kids return to where they started.

When all the preteens have taken the eyedropper of water across the room, have team members take turns filling the cup with water, walking across the room, finding one of the listed psalms (or one of a team member's choice) in the Bible, and reading it aloud as a prayer while pouring the water into the bucket.

When each team member has had a chance to dribble a prayer and pour out a prayer, ask:

- **What differences do you see between David's prayers and the simple ones you prayed in this activity?**

- **What feelings could you hear behind David's requests?**

- **Why would God want our heartfelt prayers?**

- **How could your prayers be more sincere?**

> **• EXTRA IMPACT •**
> Did you know that God doesn't ask us to do what he hasn't already done first? He pours out his heart to us, too. Have students explore these passages to discover God's honest heart-cries to us: Isaiah 30:18; 42:14; 43:4; Jeremiah 31:3, 20; Hosea 11:1-9; Matthew 23:37; and Revelation 3:19-20.

 POUR OUT YOUR HEART

Now it's time for you to demonstrate your own heartfelt prayer for your preteens. You may even want to kneel as you pray. Use words describing your honest feelings. The following is a sample of an honest, heartfelt prayer. After your prayer, provide an opportunity for students to pray.

Dear Lord:
Please help me! I'm terrified of getting on that plane next week. You know how scared I am of heights. You know that I get nauseous just thinking about it.
Please be with me. I know you *will* be with me. You promised to be with me wherever I go. Help me to trust you. Amen.

THE LORD ACCEPTS YOUR GIFT

Overview: Preteens will put gifts of prayers in a wrapped box to experience God's acceptance of both good and bad emotions.

Focus Verses: "The Lord has heard my weeping....The Lord accepts my prayer" (Psalm 6:8b-9a).

Materials: You'll need Bibles, a shoe box with a lid, wrapping paper, scissors, tape, paper, pens, and copies of the "Feelings We Feel" handout (pp. 7-8).

Preparation: Wrap the box and its lid separately before the meeting.

 LIVING PSALM

Say: **Sometimes we're afraid to go to God with our feelings because we think our feelings may be too ugly for him. We think that God only accepts our praise and happy feelings.** Write a happy prayer to God on a piece of paper, read it aloud, and put it in the box. The prayer might say something like, "Dear God, I love you for the hit I got in the game last night. Amen."

Hand out paper and pens, and have preteens write happy prayers from their own personal experiences and put them in the box.

Say: **We sometimes think that God would close his heart to us if he knew how hateful we really feel about things sometimes.** On another piece of paper, write a prayer that says something like, "Dear God, I am so jealous of my sister. I hate her for getting praise last night while I sat there like an idiot. Amen." Read the prayer aloud as you write.

Fold the prayer into a paper airplane. Put the lid on the box, and throw the airplane at the box saying: **We think that kind of prayer isn't holy enough for God.** Watch the prayer ricochet off the box.

Then say: **But God understands all of our feelings. He is just waiting for you to come to him with your anger, your tears, and your fears, just as David did.** Open the box, and "land" your paper airplane in it.

Have a volunteer read aloud the Focus Verses, Psalm 6:8b-9a. Ask a few other volunteers to read aloud a few passages from some of the "imprecatory" (or cursing) Psalms, such as: Psalm 7:6; 9:20; 11:5-6; 31:6; and 35:4-8.

Say: **When you share your true self with God, you give a gift to him. And the Lord accepts your gift.** Give each person another piece of paper, and have kids write prayers to God, telling him how they feel upset or afraid about certain people or situations. Encourage them to refer to the "Feelings We Feel" handouts to pinpoint their emotions. Ask students not to sign their names on their papers, as you'll be reading them aloud.

When preteens are finished writing their prayers, have them make their prayers into paper airplanes and land them in the box. Put the lid on the box, and repeat the Focus Verse to show that God accepts these kinds of prayers, too.

• EXTRA IMPACT •

Keep the prayer box in the room and ask the kids to put prayers in it regularly. Read aloud Psalm 55:22a: "Cast your cares upon the Lord and he will sustain you." Encourage kids to practice writing and "casting" their prayers upon the Lord.

 ## POUR OUT YOUR HEART

Open the box, and read the prayers aloud. Don't read any details that are so specific they could embarrass someone. End with a prayer like this one:

Dear Lord:
You hear our crying, our anger, and our fears. You accept our happy and unhappy prayers. Thank you for being a God we can be completely honest with. Thank you for David, who gave us examples of how we can pray. Amen.

SHARING OUR BURDENS WITH OUR BROTHERS

Overview: Preteens will use a backpack and a load of books to explore the dynamics of sharing problems in safe relationships.

Focus Verses: "My guilt has overwhelmed me like a burden too heavy to bear" (Psalm 38:4).

"My eyes will be on the faithful in the land, that they may dwell with me; he whose walk is blameless will minister to me" (Psalm 101:6).

Materials: You'll need Bibles; newsprint, tape, and a marker or a dry-erase board and marker; pens; paper; and a backpack and three heavy books for every four people.

Preparation: Write the following on a dry-erase board or newsprint and put it where students can see it:

"Safe" people will…

• accept you just the way you are,

• listen to you and care about you,

• be people you can trust,

• allow you to be yourself,

• love God and try to follow what the Bible says,

• be honest with you and let you be honest with them, and

• not share your secrets with other people.

 ## LIVING PSALM

Share this story from Joan Jacob's book, *Feelings.* Say: **A little girl complained of feeling lonely in her bedroom at night. When her father said, "But Jesus is here, Judy," she replied, "I know it, Daddy, but I want somebody with skin on." It is God's intention—part of his plan—that we get help from people with "skin on."**

We need to share our struggles with God, but we also need to share with people. Who can you share your struggles with? We all need people we can talk to. Who are the best people to take our problems to?

Point out the information about safe people on the newsprint or dry-erase board. Read through it with the preteens.

Have preteens form groups of four. Ask each person to think of a personal problem he or she is dealing with. Give each person three pieces of paper and a pen, and ask him or her to write that problem on each piece of paper. For example, someone might write, "I want to quit my piano lessons, but my mom won't be happy."

Then have each group select one person to go first by placing each of the three pieces of paper inside one of the three books, putting the books in the backpack, and putting the backpack on. The other three people on the team can pose as safe people. Ask the burden-bearer to read the Focus Verses, Psalm 38:4 and 101:6, aloud.

Then say: **Keeping our problems to ourselves is like carrying a heavy burden around. Hand a book to each person in your group as you tell that person what your problem is and how you feel about it. You'll see how sharing the burden makes it lighter—how "the faithful in the land" will minister to you.** Ask the people receiving the books to say, "I hear what you're saying. I'm here for you."

Continue this way until each group member has had a chance to be the burden-bearer. Then ask:

- **How did you feel after you shared your burden?**

- **Why do you think God designed us to need other people?**

- **What will you do the next time you have a problem?**

Give each person three more pieces of paper, and ask kids to write letters to three people, asking them to be safe people they can go to when they need help. Suggest that kids refer to the qualities you listed as they write their letters. A letter may sound something like this: "Dear Derik, I need to talk to you sometime about my problems. Will you listen to me without worrying about the bad in me? Will you keep my secrets and be a friend to me? I would like to do the same for you. Thank you! Chris" (You may want to write the example letter on the board as a template for students to copy from directly if they choose.)

Encourage preteens to give the letters to their safe people. You may want to volunteer to be a safe person for a preteen struggling to name one.

 ## POUR OUT YOUR HEART

Gather all the problems into one Bible opened to Psalm 101. Have kids pray this prayer with you.

Dear Lord:
Thank you for being someone we can turn to with all of our problems. Thank you for giving us people who we can share our troubles with. Please give us good, safe people to turn to. Please help us to be safe people for others. We love you and need you. Amen.

THE FEELING UNHAPPY PSALMS

COMPLAINT DEPARTMENT

Overview: Preteens will find God to be more than just a benign, listening ear in this skit.

Focus Verse: "Hear me, O God, as I voice my complaint; protect my life from the threat of the enemy" (Psalm 64:1).

Materials: You'll need Bibles, poster board or newsprint, markers, copies of the "Complaint Department" skit (pp. 33-34), tape, a bell, a cell phone, books, and pot holders.

Preparation: None is needed.

 LIVING PSALM

Say: **Often when we're in trouble, we go everywhere but to God for help. When we do turn to God, he does more than listen to us. He hears our complaints and acts on our behalf. We're going to act out a short skit to demonstrate that God hears your complaints.**

> ### LEADER TIP
> If you don't have a cell phone, use a toy phone or cut a phone out of cardboard.

Give each person a copy of the "Complaint Department" skit, and ask for volunteers to play the roles. The kids who don't have specific roles will be the audience. Give the actors their props, and suggest they read their lines.

Ask the other kids to use the newsprint or poster board to make signs to label the scenes: the school hall, Mrs. Dummond's classroom, the kitchen, Hans' bedroom, the school hall with the "Complaint Department" sign. Suggest they include the words of the Focus Verse, Psalm 64:1, underneath the title on the "Complaint Department" sign. Have kids decide how to set the stage and put the signs up. Then have them start the action.

When the skit is over, ask:

• **What did Hans do right in this skit? Explain.**

• **What did God do for Hans? What did Hans have to do in order for God to act?**

• **Has anyone ever bothered you the way Butch bothered Hans? What did you do about it?**

- **What can God do for you that people can't?**

Say: **Hans did the right thing by going to his teacher, his mom, and his friend. We need to share our troubles with others. But we have the special privilege of bringing our complaints to our living, active God who hears, cares, and protects us.**

 ## POUR OUT YOUR HEART

Have kids pretend to be Hans and pray the Focus Verse in past tense. For example, they might say "Dear Lord: Thank you for hearing my complaint. Thank you for bringing them to ruin. Thank you for always protecting my life. Amen."

BIG POWER IN A LITTLE WORD

Overview: Preteens will practice taking their attention off themselves and focusing on God.

Focus Verse: "But you, O Lord, sit enthroned forever" (Psalm 102:12a).

Materials: You'll need Bibles, copies of the "Feelings We Feel" handout (pp. 7-8) and the "My Secret Strategy" handout (p. 36), pens, a dry-erase board, and a marker.

Preparation: Write the following formula from "My Secret Strategy" on the dry-erase board.

"I feel_____about_____because_____. I wish I could_____,

BUT

you_____so I will_____."

LIVING PSALM

Say: **Hidden inside so many of the psalms is a tiny word made up of just three letters. Don't be fooled. There is big power in this little word.** Point to the word "but" on the board. **This little word can change how you handle a difficult situation. That's what David did, and we can do the same.**

Give each preteen a Bible, and ask several volunteers to read Psalm 102 aloud, dividing the verses among them. Have the rest of the kids follow along in their Bibles. Then have the group work together to fit the psalm into the formula written on the board. Have kids interpret the feelings of the psalmist and take turns filling in the blanks on the board according to their answers.

Then give each person a copy of "My Secret Strategy" handout and a pen, and have kids fill in the blanks to fit problems they have in their own lives. When they get to the section after "BUT you," encourage them to use their Bibles to look up a few of the psalms and include them in their prayers. For example: someone might write, **"I feel** nervous **about** going to my mom's this weekend **because** my new stepfather will be there. **I wish I could** get sick and not have to go. '**BUT** I pray to **you**, O Lord in the time of your favor; in your great love, O God, answer me with your sure salvation' (Psalm 69:13). So '**I will** praise God's name in song' (Psalm 69:30). The Lord hears me. I will go and not be afraid. **Thank you. Amen.**"

COMPLAINT DEPARTMENT

Characters:
Hans
Butch
Butch's friends
Mrs. Dummond
Hans' mom
Juan
Lady
Principal

*(**Hans** walks down the hall with his books in his hands. **Butch** comes up and pushes **Hans'** books onto the floor. **Butch** and his **buddies** circle **Hans**, taunting him and throwing wads of paper at him.)*

Butch and friends: You loser! Four-eyed freak! Cry baby!

Hans: Hey, what did you do that for?

Butch: Good job, ratting on me for cheating on the test!

Hans: I didn't rat on you.

Butch: Mrs. Dummond saw that my answers were the same as yours, and she flunked me!

Hans: It wasn't my fault. I didn't even know you could see my answers.

Butch: Sure! You're so smart you ace everything, but you didn't know I was cheatin'! You better watch your back 'cause, when you're not lookin', we're gonna do you in!

Butch's friends: Yeah!

*(The bell rings. **Butch** and his friends leave. **Hans** picks up his books, sadly. **Hans** goes to **Mrs. Dummond**.)*

Hans: Mrs. Dummond, can I talk to you?

Mrs. Dummond: I'm really busy now. What is it?

Hans: Butch is mad at me 'cause of the test.

Mrs. Dummond: Hans, I've got enough on my hands. I just can't deal with tattletales right now.

Hans: But…

Mrs. Dummond: All I can say is there better not be any more trouble between you two.

Hans: But…

Mrs. Dummond: And I better never see identical answers like that again, or you'll BOTH be in trouble.

Hans: But I didn't…

Mrs. Dummond: Go on to your next class, Hans.

Hans: *(Lowers his head and walks away.)* Yes, ma'am.

*(**Hans** goes home and finds **Mom** in the kitchen.)*

Hans: Mom, can I talk to you about something?

Mom: Sure, honey. Will you hand me the potholders?

Hans: *(Hands her the potholders.)* There's this kid at school and he…

*(The phone rings. **Mom** picks it up and "gabs" on the phone for awhile.)*

Mom: *(Puts the phone down and looks at her watch.)* Oh, no, it's 5:30! I have to take Trina to her piano lesson. Trina! Hurry up! Don't forget your book! We were late last week. We'll talk later, Hans, OK?

Hans: Yeah, I guess so.

*(Later, **Hans** and **Mom** are in Hans' bedroom.)*

Hans: Mom, can I talk to you about that kid who's been picking on me?

Mom: Sure, Hans. Wait, did you finish your volcano project? It's due tomorrow.

Hans: No, I…

Mom: Get out of bed right now, and do it! Now you'll get up late tomorrow, and I have to drive you and I'll be late for my meeting! Hans! What am I going to do with you?

*(Next day in the school hall, **Hans** goes to **Juan**.)*

Hans: Hey, Juan, I need to talk to a friend. Will you listen to me?

Juan: Sure, man—what's up?

Hans: Butch copied my answers on the test and got caught. So he and his friends started bugging me. They threatened me and called me names.

Juan: Bummer! That's the pits.

Hans: Yeah, and Mrs. Dummond won't do anything about it. Butch said he's gonna do me in. I'm kind of scared.

Juan: That stinks. I wish there was something I could do.

Hans: I guess nobody can do anything. But I feel better after talking to you.

Juan: No problem. That's what friends are for.

(They slap each other on the back.)

*(**Hans,** carrying his books with his head down, passes a lady sitting at a desk. The sign above her says: "Complaint Department.")*

Lady: Hey, kid—you got a problem?

Hans: Actually, yes, but who are you?

Lady: I just work here. Your job is to bring your problem to somebody who can do something about it. Don't you have a crowd making evil plans about you?

Hans: Why, yes.

Lady: Uh huh, read this complaint to God. *(She hands him an open Bible.)*

Hans: *(Reads Psalm 64:1-6 aloud.)* Wow, that sounds like me.

Lady: OK, here's your reply. *(She reads Psalm 64:7-9 aloud).*

Hans: You mean God would really do that for me? Aren't those Psalms just poems from a long time ago? Does God still do that kind of thing today?

Principal: *(Points to a chair.)* You sit down there, young man. I heard about your cheating. And how you and your friends threatened Hans. It seems some of your friends have realized you're not the kind of friend they need. Now we need to figure out your punishment. But first you need to do something.

Butch: *(Walks up to **Hans,** who looks scared.)* Hey man, I'm sorry for cheating off your test and threatening to beat you up. I was being stupid and got caught.

Hans: *(relieved)* It's OK. I forgive you.

Butch: *(Sees **Principal** walking to them.)* Well, I gotta go.

All kids: *(**Principal** and **Butch** walk away.)* "Let the righteous rejoice in the Lord and take refuge in him. Let all the upright in heart praise him!" (Psalm 64:10).

When preteens have finished their prayers, have them find a partner and share what they wrote. Then ask:

- **How does the word "but" change your outlook on your situation?**

- **How can this Secret Strategy make a difference in your life?**

Say: **If you'll use this Secret Strategy, you'll find your life changing for the better. Use it every day! This is the key: Look inside yourself and be honest with God about your feelings. Then look to God for strength. No matter how desperate you feel, you can always say, "BUT the Lord is still on his throne!"**

• EXTRA IMPACT •

Have each preteen write an "I feel" statement on a self-stick note and place it on himself or herself. Then have kids turn to the Psalms for "but" statements about God. See the psalms listed on "My Secret Strategy." Have the kids write these statements all over the formula on the board. For example, they may write from Psalm 10:14a "But you, O God, do see trouble and grief; you consider it to take it in hand." Then have the preteens put their self-stick notes on the board to emphasize taking their eyes off their feelings and situations and looking to God who still is on his throne!

POUR OUT YOUR HEART

Read what the group came up with from Psalm 102 as your prayer. It should read something like this:

O Lord:
I feel (tormented, anxious, and desperate). (See verses 2, 5, and 9.)
about (my pain. I don't even want to eat). (See verses 4 and 5.)
because (you are angry with me). (See verse 10.)
I feel like (a desert owl among the ruins). (See verse 6.)
I wish (I could fly away). (See verses 6 and 7.)

BUT

You, (O Lord, sit enthroned forever). (See verse 12.)
(You will arise and have compassion forever.) (See verse 13.)
So I will (praise you. I will live in your presence). (See verses 21 and 28.)

ANGRY ABOUT INJUSTICE

Overview:	Preteens will explore their feelings toward injustice and create "hope" collages.
Focus Verses:	"Do not fret when men succeed in their ways, when they carry out their wicked schemes. Refrain from anger and turn from wrath" (Psalm 37:7b-8a).
Materials:	You'll need Bibles, magazines, poster board or newsprint, scissors, and markers.
Preparation:	Gather magazines such as Newsweek, Time, U.S.News, and National Geographic (which is especially good for information about third world countries). Check with your local library or thrift shops for used copies.

MY SECRET STRATEGY

Use this handout to explore your feelings about one issue in your life. Think of an issue or situation. Then search your "Feelings We Feel" list and your heart for the words to tell God all of your feelings. You may feel many different ways about the issue. Be honest with God.

Write your own feeling and situation in the top five spaces. Then choose a psalm from the list to fill in the "but" portion. Finally, fill in the "I will" portion with your decision about what you will do with your feelings.

O Lord my God:

I feel_____

about _____

because_____

_____

I wish I could_____

BUT you_____

- Who is God, and what can he do for you? Check out the following Psalms: Psalms 3; 5; 6; 10; 13; 22; 23; 32; 34; 39; 49; 52; 55; 59; 64; 69; 71; 73; 74; 86; 91; 92; 100; 102; 106; 107; and 130. As you read, look for the words "but," and "yet." Write down the verses and references you choose.

So I will_____

Thank you! Amen.

 ## LIVING PSALM

Give each person a Bible, and have kids read aloud Psalm 37:7-11 together.

Ask:

- **How did you feel as you read these verses?**

- **Why do you think evil people hurt good people?**

Say: **It's not hard to see evil in our world. Stories about violence, war, disease, and poverty are in the news every day. We may wonder why these things exist. And we may get angry toward those who spread evil.**

It seems David may have felt the same way. In this psalm, he talks about evil people and the problems they cause.

Have kids form groups of three or four. Provide poster board or newsprint, magazines, scissors, and markers. Have kids cut out pictures of evil situations and paste them onto poster board, leaving room between the pictures to write in spaces later.

Say: **Choose verses in Psalm 37 that offer encouragement to those being hurt by evil in the pictures you chose. For example, you could copy verse 2: "For like the grass they will soon wither, like green plants they will soon die away."**

Allow preteens several minutes to write verses of encouragement around their pictures. Then ask:

- **How does writing verses of encouragement help you handle your anger toward these unjust situations?**

- **What unjust situations do you face?**

- **When you are facing unjust situations, how could this psalm offer you hope?**

POUR OUT YOUR HEART

Have preteens hold their collages and come together in a circle. Offer a prayer of hope for the people of the world being treated unjustly. Close by saying this prayer:

**Dear God,
When we see the way so many people suffer, it angers us. We ask that you would be with the suffering people of the world and you would ease their suffering. Please help us use our anger about injustice to do what we can and always trust you in the process. Help us look to you when we are being treated unjustly. Amen.**

• EXTRA IMPACT •

Before your meeting, search some Web sites for information about Christians who suffer from war, poverty, disease, or other hardships. Pass out the information to preteens. Challenge them to create words of hope from Psalm 37 to encourage these suffering people.

THE GRUDGE AS A CHERISHED PET

Overview: Preteens will nurture a "pet grudge" balloon to help them understand the hazard of harbored hatred.

Focus Verse: "Do not drag me away with the wicked, with those who do evil, who speak cordially with their neighbors but harbor malice in their hearts" (Psalm 28:3).

Materials: You'll need Bibles, markers, paper, balloons, a baby blanket or towel, and a baby bottle.

Preparation: Make fancy, folded invitations that read: "Please come to my pity party to see my pet grudge." Make an invitation for each preteen in your group.

LIVING PSALM

Hand everyone an invitation. Explain that the purpose of a "pity party" is that people will feel sorry for you. Blow up a balloon, and draw an angry face on it. Then wrap your balloon "grudge" in blanket or a towel. Introduce your pet balloon as Grudge. Pretend to feed Grudge with a baby bottle as you explain that a "grudge" is anger we want to keep alive by remembering over and over again something hurtful that was said or done to us. Tell kids that keeping anger or hatred alive this way is often called "nursing a grudge."

Write on the balloon "Jennifer teased me about my new glasses in front of Colin." Then show your pet grudge to preteens, one at a time. After each person hears about the awful incident, he or she should respond by saying something like, "She didn't!" "Poor you," "What's her problem?" or "Aren't you amazing for putting up with such a creepy friend for so long!"

Give each person a Bible, and have students read Psalm 28:3 aloud together. Define "malice" as the hatred that grows from "nursing" anger.

Ask:

- **Who does David say is wicked or evil here? Why do you think he says this?**

- **Why would anyone want to harbor malice (or keep grudges)?**

- **Why is it a problem to harbor malice or carry a grudge against someone?**

Say: **Sometimes we want to keep our anger alive because it's our way of making life "fair." We think things like, "He hurt me, so I need to hurt him back by remembering what he did." But the problem is that, although we start out by holding the anger, before you know it, it's holding us.**

Rub the balloon on your hair and let the static electricity hold it to your head. Then say: **I look pretty silly walking around with this grudge attached to me, don't I?**

According to this verse, God says we're equals with the wicked and evil if we keep grudges.

Ask:

- **Grudges can become very precious to us. How can we get rid of them?**

Say: **Forgiveness is the key.** Write on the balloon, "Lord, I forgive Jennifer for laughing at me." Pop the balloon by squeezing it or stepping on it, and say: **Our angry feelings may not disappear as fast as I popped this balloon. But if we keep on asking God to help us forgive, he'll keep on answering. That's the kind of prayer God loves to hear.**

Have each preteen blow up a balloon and find a partner. Have partners take turns sharing memories of hurtful incidents that they've carried around as grudges.

POUR OUT YOUR HEART

Have partners write on the balloons a few words about the hurtful incidents they remember. Then ask them to write prayers asking God to help them forgive and let go of the grudge. Kids can pray their prayers silently. Then have kids all pop their balloons by stepping on them or squeezing them at the same time.

PRESCRIPTION FOR ANGER

Overview: Preteens will eat jelly bean "pills" as they go through the steps to alleviate anger.

Focus Verse: "In your anger, do not sin" (Psalm 4:4a).

Materials: You'll need Bibles, pens, and six different colors of jelly beans, resealable plastic bags, permanent markers, pens, and copies of the "Anger Prescription Rx" handout (p. 41).

Preparation: None is needed.

LIVING PSALM

Say: **God created us in his image. God gets angry. When he came to earth as Jesus, he became furious. Anger is part of being human. Being angry is not a sin; it's what you do with your anger that could be a sin. God understands our anger, but he gave us some rules for dealing with it.**

Give each person a Bible, and read Psalm 4:4a aloud together. Give each person a resealable plastic bag, a permanent marker, a pen, and an "Anger Prescription Rx" handout. Have kids turn their handouts over and write the following two rules: (1) "Don't hurt anybody" and (2) "Don't hurt anything." Explain that hurting people entails both physical and verbal offenses.

Then have each preteen use a permanent marker to write the words of the Focus Verse, Psalm 4:4a, on their plastic bags.

Say: **Anger isn't a sin; it's a feeling. But when we keep it bottled for long, it can become destructive. The Bible instructs us in Ephesians 4:31 to get rid of our anger. God's Word has the answer to our problems. Tucked inside Psalm 4 is a prescription for getting rid of anger.**

Have kids form pairs and read through Psalm 4:4-8 together. Then have them write next to the steps on their "Anger Prescription Rx" handouts words from the Psalm that match the step. For example, number four says "Ask for forgiveness." A preteen might write "Offer right sacrifices."

When kids are finished, set out the jelly beans, and have pairs work together to match jelly bean colors to the steps in the anger prescription and write each color next to the rule on the handout. For example, preteens may choose red for identified anger, blue for not hurting anyone, purple for searching their hearts, green for carrying a grudge, and yellow for turning to God. Have kids fold the handouts and tuck them into the plastic bags along with several jelly bean "doses."

Ask:

- **What boundaries does God set on our anger?**

- **What is the hardest part of this prescription for you? Why?**

- **How can you focus your anger in a positive way?**

 ## POUR OUT YOUR HEART

Have kids eat the jelly beans, according to how they decided the colors correspond to the prescription, as you pray this prayer aloud.

Dear Lord:
Sometimes we get angry. In our anger, please help us to not sin. Help us to honestly search our hearts to own our part of the problem. Forgive us when our anger turns into hate. You fill our hearts with joy. Help us to act and feel peaceful as we trust in you. Amen.

OF FOOLS AND FURY

Overview: Preteens will see the folly of revenge in the story of David and Nabal.

Focus Verse: "Wait for the Lord and keep his way. He will exalt you to inherit the land; when the wicked are cut off, you will see it" (Psalm 37:34).

Materials: You'll need Bibles; a stretchy, one-size-fits-all glove; and copies of the "Of Fools and Fury" script (pp. 43-44).

Preparation: None is needed.

 ## LIVING PSALM

Say: **Psalm 37 is kind of like this glove; it's a one-size-fits-all psalm.** Pass the glove around so preteens can try it on. Say: **This psalm fits so many situations. We don't know exactly what situation David was in when he wrote it. But we often share the same feelings.**

Give each preteen a Bible, and have kids take turns reading Psalm 37 aloud. Then give everyone a copy of the "Of Fools and Fury" script, and ask for volunteers to play the parts of David,

Doctor ⎯⎯⎯⎯

ANGER PRESCRIPTION RX

TO ALLEVIATE ANGER:

- ADMIT YOUR ANGER TO YOURSELF.
- DON'T HURT ANYONE OR ANYTHING.
- SEARCH YOUR HEART FOR YOUR PART OF THE PROBLEM.
- ASK FOR FORGIVENESS IF YOUR ANGER HAS TURNED INTO A GRUDGE OR HATE. FORGIVE THE ONE WHO HURT YOU.
- KEEP LOOKING TO GOD TO HELP YOU CONTROL YOUR ANGER.

Nabal, the Servant, and Abigail. The rest of the group will be the Mighty Men and Women. Have the Mighty Men and Women form two teams, and have each team take responsibility for finding two of the verses from Psalm 37 to insert in the script. Give teams a few minutes to find the verses they want to use.

Say: **Psalm 37 tells us not to fret. To fret means to worry or be annoyed. The original word David used also meant to be angry. When we see wicked people flourishing, we tend to get angry. David did. Our skit is about one of the few times in David's life when he sought revenge. It's a fascinating story, and you can be a part of it.**

> • **EXTRA IMPACT** •
>
> Give yourself and your preteens a wonderful learning experience. Give everyone three pieces of paper. Ask kids to title one piece, "I Will…" and to title the second piece, "You Will…" The third piece should be titled, "The Wicked Will…". Ask kids to go through Psalm 37 and record everything that God promises on the "You Will…" and "The Wicked Will…" sheets. Then have preteens write their part on the "I Will…" paper. Here's a short sample:
>
> | I Will... | You Will... | The Wicked Will... |
> |---|---|---|
> | Delight myself in the Lord. | give me the desires of my heart. | wither like grass |
> | Not fret | uphold me | be no more |

Have kids present the skit. When they're finished, ask:

• **What was David tempted to do? Why didn't he do it?**

• **Share a time you were tempted to take revenge. What happened?**

• **Which verse in this psalm would help you the most to wait on the Lord?**

 ## POUR OUT YOUR HEART

Have kids choose a favorite verse from Psalm 37 and personalize it. Ask preteens one at a time to pray their verses. Here's an example from verses 4 and 34:

Dear Lord my God:
I will wait for you, Lord. I will keep your way. I will delight myself in you. And you will give me the desires of my heart. Thank you. Amen.

"LEAF" IT TO GOD

Overview: Preteens will share personal enemy stories and compose prayers asking God to help them leave judgment to him.

Focus Verse: "'Because he loves me,' says the Lord, 'I will rescue him.'" (Psalm 91:14a).

Materials: You'll need Bibles; newsprint, tape, and a marker or a dry-erase board and marker; cardboard; scissors; paper; crayons; and copies of the "'Leaf' It to God" handout (p. 47).

Preparation: None is needed.

LIVING PSALM

No one needs to define the word "enemy" for an early adolescent. If you haven't been to school lately, you'd be shocked to find out that kids have listed the things they deal with (in

OF FOOLS AND FURY

(from 1 Samuel 25)

Characters:
David
Nabal
Servant
Abigail
Mighty Men and Women

Setting:

David has just moved to the desert with his men. He's heard of a wealthy man named Nabal who also lives in the desert.

David: We're starving in this desert. Let's go ask Nabal for food. It's sheep-shearing season, and he has more than three thousand sheep.

Mighty Men and Women: [Insert a verse from Psalm 37.]

David: True, but we can't feed six hundred men on these berries and lizards. You ten men go to Nabal, wish him well, and ask him for some food.

Mighty Men and Women: *(to Nabal)* We greet you in David's name. We'd like some food, please—and remember that we've been protecting your shepherds.

Nabal: *(rudely)* Who is David? There's a lot of riff-raff around today! Why should I give up my bread and my water and my meat for strangers? Forget it—scram!

Mighty Men and Women: *(to David)* He said "no." [Insert a verse from Psalm 37.]

David: Put on your swords. God help me if by morning I leave alive one male in Nabal's household!

Mighty Men and Women: Don't do it, David. [Insert a verse from Psalm 37.]

David: I'm furious! I helped that fool, and he paid me back with evil. Let's go, men—I'm going with you. Two hundred of you stay with the supplies.

Servant: *(to Abigail)* Abigail, because of your wicked, foolish husband, David is coming to destroy our household. Think fast, lady! We're in trouble.

Abigail: Quickly, help me load these loaves of bread, raisin cakes, and sheep meat onto these donkeys. Let's go! And don't tell my husband.

Servant: All this food?

Abigail: Why, yes. *(To David)* Please don't take revenge!

David: Praise be to the Lord! You have kept me from taking revenge. Go home in peace. And thank you for the food.

(Abigail leaves.)

Abigail: *(to Nabal)* You should know that David almost destroyed our household but I stopped him with words of wisdom.

Nabal: You what!? How could you, you….*(Clutches his heart and pretends to die.)*

Servant: *(to Abigail)* He's dead.

Mighty Men and Women: *(to David)* Guess what? Nabal's dead! Good thing you didn't sin against the Lord by taking revenge. [Insert a verse from Psalm 37 here.]

Abigail and David: *(Abigail links arms with David.)* Delight yourself in the Lord, and he will give you the desires of your heart.

their own words) as: getting pushed, kicked, body slammed, spit at, having stuff shoved down their backs, being given "wedgies" in front of the class, choked, having fingers poked in their eyes, being sniffed under their armpits, and having their heads stuck into toilets. All of this is comes on top of verbal taunts and cursing.

Take the time to ask your preteens the following questions. Don't judge any of their answers; just listen, and record their responses on a dry-erase board or newsprint.

Ask:

- **Do other people ever cut you down? If so, why?**

- **Do you ever feel as though you're not allowed to be different? Explain.**

- **Tell me about a time someone at school hurt you. Why did this happen?**

- **Do other students ever pick on you? What do they do?**

- **Do other students call you names? If so, what are they?**

- **How do you feel about the way your enemies treat you?**

- **What would you like to do to your enemies?**

- **What do you actually do to your enemies?**

- **What would happen if you told a teacher or another adult about this?**

Say: **It can be a vicious world. It was for David, too. He spent much of his life escaping his enemies, and, along the way, he wrote prayers called the psalms. Almost half of the Psalms are about dealing with enemies. We are sometimes surprised at David's honesty. He wanted his enemies dead, but, except in battle, didn't end their lives himself. For example, although he had opportunities, he wouldn't lift his hand against King Saul, who was out to kill him. David told God how he felt, and he asked God for his help against his enemies. Then he waited. And God came through for him! David learned how to leave his problems with God.**

Ask:

- **Do you think you could leave your problems with God? Why or why not?**

- **What would it mean to leave your problems with God?**

Give each preteen a Bible, and ask a volunteer to read Psalm 91:14-16 aloud while the others follow along. Then give each person a "'Leaf' It to God" handout, cardboard, scissors, paper, and crayons. Have kids cut their leaves out, trace them onto the cardboard, and cut out the cardboard leaves. Then have them place the leaves on a piece of blank paper and rub the side of a crayon across the edges of the cardboard using a variety of fall colors. When kids lift the cardboard leaves, they'll have white leaves surrounded by colors. Each person should have about eight leaves on his or her paper.

Have preteens title their papers, "Don't Take Revenge. 'Leaf' It to God!" Then have preteens compose personalized prayers inside the leaves, using the six "I will" promises found in Psalm 91:14-16. Tell preteens to change each promise into a personalized prayer and then add the words "I leave it to you, Lord." For example, one leaf might read, "You will be with me when I am in trouble. I leave it to you, Lord."

POUR OUT YOUR HEART

Ask if anyone would like to read his or her prayer aloud. If not, use this prayer based on Psalm 91:14-26.

Dear Lord:
I love you. I know you will rescue me. I leave my problem to you. I do stand up for you. I know you will protect me. I leave my problem to you. You will answer me. I leave my problem with you. You will be with me. I leave my problem to you. You will deliver and honor me. I leave my problem with you. You will satisfy me. I leave my problem to you. I trust you. Amen.

"FEAR NOT" MEDIA CAMPAIGN

Overview: Preteens will develop commercials and advertisements to encourage others to trust in God.

Focus Verses: "I lie down and sleep; I wake again, because the Lord sustains me. I will not fear the tens of thousands drawn up against me on every side" (Psalm 3:5-6).

Materials: You'll need Bibles, poster board, markers, paper, a cassette recorder with a blank cassette, and copies of the "Fear-busters" handout (p. 49).

Preparation: None is needed.

LIVING PSALM

Say: **Fear can drive us even more powerfully than our loves or hates.** Ask:

- **What are some things you're afraid of?**

- **What are some different forms of fear?**

- **Why can we be brave in the face of terrifying circumstances?**

Say: **We can't tell people not to be afraid, because we can't tell people how to feel. But we can give people a reason to be brave. If a child is afraid of what's in the closet, his or her mom may open the closet door to prove there's nothing in there. God tells us to not be afraid—and for good reason. You're going to find those reasons as we develop a "Fear Not" advertising blitz.**

Preteens will be developing various types of ads and announcements to tout their God "product" as the solution to the problem of fear, using any verses they choose from the "Fear-Busters" handouts.

Have the group form four teams. Explain that each team will develop one type of advertisement to demonstrate God's ability to solve the problem of fear. Give each team a "Fear-Busters" handout, paper, and markers, and tell teams they are to use at least one of the verses from the

'Leaf' It
to God

• EXTRA IMPACT •

Show the preteens how to use a concordance to look up passages about fear. Look under "afraid," "fear," "distress," and "cry." (Explain that they should ignore those verses that talk about fearing the Lord.) Tell your students that there are 365 'fear nots' in the Bible, one for each day of the year.

handout in whatever they develop. Encourage kids to find additional 'fear-buster' psalms. Assign each team one of the following tasks: write a one-minute TV commercial, use the poster board to make a billboard, use the tape recorder to make a one-minute radio advertisement, and design door-to-door fliers. Encourage the kids to come up with the ideas on their own. If they need some help, refer to the following ideas:

Here's a sample radio advertisement:

Reporter: This word just in from WNIV: There is an earthquake rocking the San Salista Valley. It measured 6.7 on the Richter scale. So far we haven't seen the complete damage. We can see from our helicopter that a building under construction collapsed. No fatalities are recorded yet. Seismic activity…Pardon me, this just in, "Therefore we will not fear, though the earth give way and the mountains fall into the heart of the sea" (Psalm 46:2). Say, what is this?

Voice: It's true, "God is our refuge and strength, an ever-present help in trouble. The Lord Almighty is with us" (Psalm 46:1, 7a).

Reporter: Even during times of tragedy like this?

Voice: Yes, "The Lord Almighty is with us; the God of Jacob is our fortress" (Psalm 46:11).

Reporter: Well, it's good to know that even during our trouble and tragedy, the Lord is with us, up in the helicopter or down in the valley below. Stay tuned for the next WNIV update.

The TV commercial might show a problem that would cause a preteen to be afraid, such as going to a new school. This commercial could use Psalm 118:6 as the solution and show one person holding hands with an invisible God.

If the billboard team gets stuck, suggest using Psalm 56:9 and show enemies running from a Christian.

The kids developing fliers might pretend they have a business called Fearbusters, Inc. and use Psalm 34:4 to advertise it. They could include references from people who have already have sought the Lord and been answered.

POUR OUT YOUR HEART

Have the preteens each take a verse from the "Fear-Busters" handout and personalize it for the prayer time. Use this sample from Psalm 34:4 to show them how to change the words to more modern words.

Dear Lord:
I looked for you. I needed you, and you answered me. Thank you. You rescued me from all my fears. And you will tomorrow. I love you. I need you. Amen.

FEAR-BUSTERS

- "I lie down and sleep; I wake again, because the Lord sustains me. I will not fear the tens of thousands drawn up against me on every side" (Psalm 3:5-6).

- "I will fear no evil, for you are with me" (Psalm 23:4b).

- "The Lord is my light and my salvation—whom shall I fear? The Lord is the stronghold of my life—of whom shall I be afraid?
  Though an army besiege me, my heart will not fear; though war break out against me, even then will I be confident" (Psalm 27:1, 3).

- "I sought the Lord, and he answered me; he delivered me from all my fears" (Psalm 34:4).

- "Therefore we will not fear, though the earth give way and the mountains fall into the heart of the sea" (Psalm 46:2).

- "God is our refuge and strength, an ever-present help in trouble. The Lord Almighty is with us" (Psalm 46:1, 7a).

- "Why should I fear when evil days come, when wicked deceivers surround me?" (Psalm 49:5)

- "Evening, morning and noon, I cry out in distress, and he hears my voice. He ransoms me unharmed from the battle waged against me, even though many oppose me" (Psalm 55:17-18).

- "When I am afraid, I will trust in you. In God, whose word I praise, in God I trust; I will not be afraid. What can mortal man do to me?" (Psalm 56:3-4).

- "Then my enemies will turn back when I call for help. By this I will know that God is for me" (Psalm 56:9).

- "You will not fear the terror of night, nor the arrow that flies by day...for he will command his angels concerning you to guard you in all your ways" (Psalm 91:5, 11).

- "[A righteous man] will have no fear of bad news; his heart is steadfast, trusting in the Lord. His heart is secure, he will have no fear" (Psalm 112:7-8a).

- "The Lord is with me; I will not be afraid" (Psalm 118:6a).

DISASTER 911

Overview: Preteens will practice a tornado drill and turn to God for relief from fear.

Focus Verses: "Have mercy on me, O God, have mercy on me, for in you my soul takes refuge. I will take refuge in the shadow of your wings until the disaster has passed. I cry out to God Most High, to God, who fulfills his purpose for me" (Psalm 57:1-2).

Materials: You'll need Bibles; newsprint, tape, and a marker or a dry-erase board and marker; and copies of the "911—Psalms to the Rescue!" handout (pp. 21-22). If you have them, provide flashlights and battery-powered radios, as well.

Preparation: Write the following tornado procedures on newsprint or a dry-erase board:

- Watch for a tornado when it hails or the sky turns green.

- Turn a battery-powered radio to a station broadcasting weather, and grab a flashlight (if you have time).

- Take refuge in an interior room, and stay away from windows.

- Take refuge under a sturdy table until the disaster has passed.

- Crouch down. Cover your head.

 ## LIVING PSALM

Say: **Today we're going to discuss dealing with disaster. Have any of you ever been in or seen a natural disaster? The disaster we're going to deal with right now is a tornado!**

Have preteens practice going through a tornado drill by following the safety rules written on the newsprint or dry-erase board. While kids are hiding under the tables, turn out the lights, and suggest that kids use flashlights, if you have them.

Say: **Hiding from a killer tornado reminds me of David, hiding in his cave. He said, "I will take refuge in the shadow of your wings until the disaster has passed." Imagine for a moment that we're not taking refuge from a random twister but from three thousand of King Saul's soldiers—out to get David's head. David and his six hundred men are holding their breath in a huge cave. They know Saul is close. Is David drawing up battle plans? Practicing with his sword? Organizing his men into battalions? No. David was probably praying.**

Give each student a Bible, and ask volunteers to take turns reading Psalm 57 aloud while others follow along. Ask:

- **What do you think David felt when he wrote Psalm 57:1-2?**

- **What did David compare himself to in verse 1?**

- **Can any of you share a time you felt this scared?**

- **Which of these verses would help to calm your panic in a disaster?**

Have preteens come out from under the tables, and say: **Did God come through for David? You bet he did! He came through in a way that David never would have dreamed of. King Saul actually came into the cave to go to the bathroom. The men were begging David to kill him. But David said, "I will not lift my hand. I will not take revenge. The Lord will make it right for me." Did he? You bet he did! David cut off a corner of Saul's robe instead of his head. When the king realized that David had spared his life, he took his soldiers and went home. The disaster had passed.**

Ask:

- **What's the first thing we should do in a real disaster?**

Say: **Usually the first thing we should do in a disaster is call 911 for help. When you call, the dispatchers are trained to calm you down. You aren't just saying, "I'm scared" into the air. You're talking to someone who can actually help you.**

Give each preteen a "911—Psalms to the Rescue!" handout, and have kids form pairs. Have pairs read any verses of their choosing. Ask them to share times they felt the way the psalmist must have when he wrote each psalm.

 ## POUR OUT YOUR HEART

Have preteens go through Psalm 57 and use it to create a disaster drill, making up a list of "safety procedures" to follow in times of fear. Then they can pray it back to God. If you have time, show them how this psalm, like so many, fits into the Secret Strategy Prayer Pattern. Your prayer time may look like this:

> **O God:**
> **I cry out to you.**
> **I hide in your protective power.**
> **I remember I am talking to you who can save me.**
> **This is my situation:** [fill in a specific situation here].
> **I praise you. Let your glory be over all the earth.**
> **So I will sing of your love.**
> **Amen.**

DRAGON OF DELIVERANCE

Overview: Preteens will look at Psalm 18 in the light of a modern story to see how God is still our "dragon of deliverance."

Focus Verses: "Smoke rose from his nostrils; consuming fire came from his mouth, burning coals blazed out of it. He parted the heavens and came down; dark clouds were under his feet. He mounted the cherubim and flew; he soared on the wings of the wind" (Psalm 18:8a, 9a, 10).

Materials: You'll need Bibles, pens, and copies of the "Dragon of Deliverance" handout (p. 54).

Preparation: None is needed.

 LIVING PSALM

Say: **When you're having a problem, it's important to recognize your feelings and share them. When you ask God to step in, you aren't just processing your feelings. You are talking to your Lord. You are talking to someone who can help you. He will help you if you'll ask him and believe him and wait patiently for him.**

> ### LEADER TIP
> The imagery in this Psalm is incredible—an artist's dream! Before you hand out the "Dragon of Deliverance" handouts, ask for volunteer artists to draw their own dragons while Psalm 18:7-15 is read.

Give each preteen a Bible, and ask kids to open their Bibles to Psalm 18. Tell this story: **Ivan was excited to finally play ball this year. He had wanted to play ever since he was in second grade. At first, his family couldn't afford it. The next year, his family moved. Then his mom's work schedule changed, and then Ivan broke his arm. Finally, this year, things worked out so Ivan could play. When he looked into the mirror at his green and gold Dragons uniform, he held his head high and smiled. His mom smiled too. "Mom," Ivan said, "I'm a little nervous about playing ball this year. You know all the kids have been in a league since they were in kindergarten."**

"Don't worry. You're a good hitter—and remember, it's just for fun anyway."

"I hope the other players know that," Ivan replied.

That first practice was a disaster. Ivan missed an easy pop fly. Then he missed a grounder that was coming right to him. And he struck out both times he was up to bat. "You couldn't hit the side of a barn," Andy hissed at Ivan.

After practice when the coach was gone, Andy, Eric, and Cody surrounded Ivan as he was tying his shoe. "Loser," Cody shoved him. "You're gonna make us lose the trophy this year. Let's break his arm so we get him off our team!"

Andy and Cody dumped ice water down Ivan's back. Then they kicked him. Ivan fell to his knees, wiping the tears from his eyes. "I'm gonna tell my dad!" he yelled.

"Cry baby's gonna tell daddy!" the others jeered.

"Hey," Ivan thought, "I am going to tell my other father. God," he prayed, "I need you!"

Ask preteens to read a verse each from Psalm 18:7-15. Ask each preteen to stand up as you point to him or her, read the verse, and then sit down.

Continue the story: **Andy, Cody, and Eric heard a strange sound in the sky. They looked up to see a fierce, fire-breathing, mountain-shaking, heart-stopping monster with smoke flaring from his nostrils riding on powerful angels. "Ahh," they screamed. "What's that?" They turned and ran.**

Ivan got up, brushing the dirt off his pants. Then he practiced and practiced. During the tournament, he hit a grand slam that won the game. "How did you do it?" his teammates wanted to know. Ivan said:

Have preteens choose verses from Psalm 18 that would fit here. Good verses to choose might be: 17, 18, 19, 27, 34, or 35.

After the story, ask:

- **Do you think God can really do that for us today? Can you share a time God rescued you or someone you know?**

- **What do we have to do to wake up our "dragon of deliverance"?** (See Psalm 18:6, 20-26).

- **Why do we sometimes rely on ourselves instead of crying out to God?**

POUR OUT YOUR HEART

Give each preteen a copy of the "Dragon of Deliverance" handout and a pen. Have each person write a prayer on the dragon by personalizing verses choosen from Psalm 18. A prayer might sound like this:

Dear Dragon of Deliverance:
When I am in distress, I will call to you, my God, for help. My cry will come before you into your ears. You will part the heavens for me. You will soar on the wings of the wind. You can shoot arrows at my enemies. You will take hold of me and rescue me. I exalt you, oh God, my Savior! Amen.

THE GOD I CAN'T GET RID OF

Overview: Preteens will see how Psalm 118 might answer their prayers. Then they'll make foot pads to remind them of God's invisible, constant presence.

Focus Verse: "The Lord is with me; I will not be afraid" (Psalm 118:6a).

Materials: You'll need Bibles; paper; newsprint, tape, and a marker or a dry-erase board and marker. You'll also need scissors, a sheet of thin craft foam, and a pen or permanent marker for each person.

Preparation: Write the following script on the newsprint or dry-erase board.

Lydia: God, I'm scared. Actually, I'm terrified. I have to give this report in front of the whole class, and I'm afraid I'll forget my lines.

God: I hear your anguish. You are doing the right thing, crying out to me (verse 5).

Lydia: Lord, I've always messed up when I've had to speak out loud.

God: I am with you. Don't be afraid. And besides, what can the kids do to you (verse 6)?

Lydia: They could laugh at me.

God: I am with you. I will be your helper (verse 7).

DRAGON OF DELIVERANCE

Lydia: Promise, Lord?

God: I promise to be with you. I promise to help you. You will triumph. Trust me; you'll do a great job (verse 7).

Lydia: Maybe I should have my partner, Shayleen, do this part of the report?

God: It's better to trust in me than to trust in people. I will come through for you (verse 8).

Lydia: OK, God. I believe you. I trust you. You are my strength (verse 14). I feel a lot more positive about that report tomorrow. You are my God, and I will give you thanks. You are my God, and I will exalt you! (verse 28). Amen.

 ## LIVING PSALM

Give each preteen a Bible, and have kids read Psalm 118:5-7 together. Ask:

- **What does "anguish" mean?**

- **When you're afraid, which part of these verses might help you?**

- **Why is it so hard to feel certain that the Lord is with us?**

Say: **We want to see God. We want to touch God. We want to hear God talking aloud to us. But we can't. All we can do is believe and remember that God is with us. He loves us. He is always with us. He promised it, so we know it's true.**

> ● **EXTRA IMPACT** ●
>
> Tell kids that we can't entirely escape fear. Even David was afraid. Ask kids to look up 1 Samuel 21:12. Explain that we can't control our feelings; we can only control what we do with those feelings. Heroes aren't people whose palms never sweat and hearts never pound. They are people who do what they are afraid to do *with* sweaty palms, pounding hearts, and praying lips!

Give each person a sheet of craft foam, a pen or permanent marker, and scissors. Ask the preteens to take off their shoes and trace both feet onto the craft foam. Then have them cut out the foot outlines. They may need to cut the outlines a bit smaller so that the craft-foam shapes will fit inside their shoes.

Then have each person write on one foot shape, "Lord, you are with me." Have kids write, "I will not be afraid" (Psalm 118:6b) on the other shape.

When they're finished, say: **Put these foam pads in your shoes, and wear them wherever you go. The softness will give you comfort; the message will give you strength. In times of fear, remember what's under you, who is inside you, and who is beside you. The Lord is with you! Do not be afraid!**

 ## POUR OUT YOUR HEART

This is the perfect opportunity to teach the preteens how to have a written conversation with God. Their walk with God will be much richer when they practice this kind of conversation. Remind the preteens that complete honesty with God is the key.

Give the preteens paper, and have them read through "Lydia's prayer" on the board. Ask them to find and copy the verses included as references in Lydia's prayer. Then ask them to write out their own talks with God. You can pray the prayer aloud with the group.

BODYGUARD GAME

Overview: Preteens will read David's "temporary insanity" story and play a game similar to dodge ball.

Focus Verse: "The angel of the Lord encamps around those who fear him, and he delivers them" (Psalm 34:7).

Materials: You'll need Bibles, table-tennis balls or foam balls, and permanent markers.

Preparation: None is needed.

LIVING PSALM

Psalm 34 is a companion to an unusual story about David. Read aloud this version of 1 Samuel 21:10–22:1:

King Saul wanted David dead. So David fled, hiding in fields, caves, and with a priest. Then David thought he had a smart plan: "I'll go hide among our enemy, the Philistines. Saul will never look for me there!" So he went to Achish, king of Gath.

Now, it may have seemed like a good idea at the time, but David forgot how popular he was. Remember that David killed the giant Goliath, the Philistine's prized fighter, in front of the entire army. David became a hero, and that's why Saul was so jealous of him. King Achish was thrilled to have an Israelite traitor join him, but some of his servants weren't so gullible. They asked, "Isn't this David...the one they sing about in their dances: 'Saul has slain his thousands and David his tens of thousands'?" Achish's servants grabbed David.

Let's stop here and think about David. Ask:

• **What is David up against here?**

• **It's possible that no one even knows where David is. Who could rescue him?**

• **David had made fools of the Philistines. What might they do to him?**

• **How would you feel if you were in David's sandals?**

Say: **The Bible says David was "very much afraid." What could David do? How could he get away? Where was God? He couldn't even sweet-talk his way out of this one. Let's turn to Psalm 34:4, 6, and 17.** Give kids Bibles, and have them look up the verses and read them aloud.

Say: **David's prayer probably didn't sound very eloquent. It may have sounded something like, "Help! God, I need you!" And God sent an angel to help. David suddenly had a brilliant idea.** Have kids read 1 Samuel 21:13–22:1. Say: **This passage tells us the king actually drove David away. Can't you just see David wiping the spit off his beard as he runs for home, laughing and praising God? I think he couldn't wait to find a cave and write this psalm.**

LEADER TIP

If you don't have access to table-tennis balls or foam balls, make your own balls by crumpling up aluminum foil inside sheets of paper.

Have preteens play Bodyguard. To play, one volunteer needs to act the part of the assailant and another needs to act the part of David. The assailant's job is to try to hit "David" with table-tennis balls as "David"

walks from one side of the room to the other. The rest of the group will need to huddle around "David" and act as Angel-of-the-Lord bodyguards. Their job is to protect "David" from the assailant's attacks. As they cross the room in a huddle, the Angel-of-the-Lord bodyguards should repeat the Focus Verse, Psalm 34:7, over and over. Have preteens take turns playing David, the Angel-of-the-Lord bodyguards, and the assailant.

 ## POUR OUT YOUR HEART

Give each preteen a ball. Have kids use permanent markers to write the words of the Focus Verse on their balls. Then have them pray this prayer with you.

Dear Lord:
You are amazing! You can get us out of bad situations in ways we'd never dream of! You send an angel to protect us. Thank you. We will cry to you for help. You will answer us. Help us when we're afraid to trust in you. Amen.

THE PRETTY WOMAN WITH THE MUSTACHE

Overview: Preteens will draw mustaches on magazine models to help them become aware of their own sin.

Focus Verse: "For in his own eyes he flatters himself too much to detect or hate his sin" (Psalm 36:2).

Materials: You'll need Bibles; a newsprint, tape, and a marker or a dry erase board and marker; a hand mirror; black markers; paper; scissors; glue sticks; and pages from magazines or catalogs that show models.

Preparation: Check the preteen suitability of the content on both sides of the pages before bringing them to class.

LIVING PSALM

Draw a mustache on a picture of a model. Hold the picture in front of your face, and hold a mirror so that the picture is reflected. Then describe how gorgeous "you" are. For example, you might say: **"I just can't believe how beautiful I am! Don't I have perfectly arched eyebrows; a perfectly shaped mouth; and straight, pearly teeth? My hair just *shines*, and my complexion is *sooo* creamy. Don't you think I'm just perfect?"** When a preteen asks you about the mustache, say: **"What mustache?"**

Ask:

- **How could a beautiful model miss her own mustache?**

- **What do you think the mustache represents?**

- **How can we use God's word as a mirror to see our own sins—or mustaches?**

Read the Focus Verse, Psalm 36:2, aloud as you write it on the dry erase board or newsprint. Define the words "flatter" and "detect." Say: **It's easy for us to see everyone else's sin and not see our own. But be careful about pointing a finger at someone else's sin; you'll find three fingers are pointing back at you!**

> **• EXTRA IMPACT •**
>
> Summarize the story of David and Bathsheba for your group. Then have kids turn to 2 Samuel 12:1-13 and take turns reading the verses aloud. Ask:
>
> - **Why didn't David see himself in Nathan's story?**

Have kids form pairs, and give each pair a few magazine or catalog pages and a black marker. Have partners find pictures of beautiful women, draw mustaches on the pictures, and use each other as "mirrors" as they describe the model's beauty.

Then have each preteen describe his or her own real attributes and admit to a "mustache" or two. For example, one partner might say to another, "I am great at art. I care a lot about people. I'm good at following directions. But I get stingy with sharing my bedroom when my brother's friends are over, and I have a hard time not teasing Corey."

 ## POUR OUT YOUR HEART

Give everyone scissors, a glue stick, and a piece of paper. Have kids cut out their mustache pictures and glue them on paper, leaving room to write the Focus Verse and a prayer. Have each preteen write a prayer to God by putting the Focus Verse into his or her own words. Read your own aloud, or use the one below as an example:

> **Dear Lord my God:**
> **Sometimes I think I'm so wonderful that I don't realize I have sin as obvious as a mustache. Please help me to see my own sin. Help me to hate my sin. Thank you for forgiving me. Amen.**

SIN: THE WALL OF SEPARATION

Overview: Preteens will form a barrier to experience how sin separates us from God.

Focus Verse: "If I had cherished sin in my heart, the Lord would not have listened" (Psalm 66:18).

Materials: You'll need Bibles, paper, self-stick notes, pens, and scissors.

Preparation: None is needed.

LIVING PSALM

Say: **Sin that we hold on to is like a wall that separates us from God.** Read Psalm 66:18 aloud. Then say: **We're going to play a game to demonstrate this. If your** prayers seem to be hitting the ceiling rather than reaching God's ears, maybe you're cherishing—or holding on to—one or more sins in your heart.

Give each person a piece of paper, scissors, a self-stick note, and a pen. Ask kids to each cut two heart shapes from the paper and fold the shapes in half. Ask them to write a prayer request on the outside of the folded hearts. The prayer request might be, "Dear Lord, please help me with my math test." Then ask each person to write a real or hypothetical sin, such as, "I cussed today," on the self-stick note. Have kids place the self-stick note inside one of the two hearts, then ask them to put their folded hearts together in a pile.

Lay an open Bible on a chair on one side of the room; the Bible will represent God. Have about half of the preteens stand shoulder-to-shoulder in front of the chair, with their backs to it to form a "wall," or a barrier to God.

Ask a volunteer to select a folded heart, walk up to the wall, and read what's written on the heart as a prayer to God. The volunteer should then open the heart and show "the wall" whether or not it's clean of sin. Explain that, if the heart is clean of sin, he or she can pass through the human "wall" and give the request to God by placing it on the Bible. If the volunteer tries to get through the wall with sin in the heart, kids in the wall need to squeeze together to block the way. Have a few volunteers try to get through the wall to God. Then ask:

- **What prevented these people from getting their requests heard by God?**

- **What can they do about it?**

Say: **Sin separates you from God. There's only one prayer that God hears through our sin-barrier, and that is, "I'm sorry." If you are cherishing sin and stubbornly not admitting it to God, your prayers will go unanswered. To be forgiven, you have to agree with God that your sin is sin and say you're sorry.**

Have each person apologize aloud for the sin that was written on the self-stick note inside his or her heart. Ask:

- **What does God do with our sin when we confess it?**

Say: **He takes it away. Just like that. His ears open up, too.** Have a volunteer throw away the self-stick note and walk through the line to lay his or her heart on the Bible. Let each person take a turn doing the same thing. Give each person a Bible, and have kids read Psalm 66:18-20 aloud together.

 ## POUR OUT YOUR HEART

Give each person another piece of paper and a new self-stick note. Have kids cut out new heart shapes and write on it their own version of Psalm 66:18-20 as a prayer. Following is a sample:

Dear Lord my God:
When I kept this sin in my heart (write the sin written on the self-stick note), **you didn't listen to me. When I said that I was sorry, you took my sin away.** (Throw away the self-stick note.) **Thank you, God, for hearing my prayer. You have not kept your love from me! Amen.**

WASH THE GUILT AWAY

Overview: Preteens will watch God's anger be washed away and see God's favor remain.

Focus Verse: "For his anger lasts only a moment, but his favor lasts a lifetime" (Psalm 30:5a).

Materials: You'll need Bibles, washable and permanent markers, foam plates, putty, and a large bowl of water.

Preparation: Try the demonstration at home ahead of time.

LIVING PSALM

Say: **It's almost too incredible to believe that when God forgives, he forgets. God is disappointed when we sin. But when we say we're sorry, God blesses us with his favor. Favor means goodwill or approval.**

Use a washable marker to write, "For his anger lasts only a moment" on a foam plate. Then, with the permanent marker, write "but his favor lasts a lifetime" (Psalm 30:5a). Say: **David could love God big-time, but he could also sin big-time. He loved a married woman. He lied, he deceived, and then to top it all off, he made sure the woman's husband was killed in battle. The Lord was angry with David in this situation. David felt guilty, a feeling God gives us so we can confess. David apologized to God, saying, "I have sinned."** Wash the plate off in the bowl, and show kids how only "the favor" remains.

• EXTRA IMPACT •

Have the preteens form five groups, and ask each group to read one of these psalms: Psalm 6, 32, 38, 51, and 103. Ask each group to talk about what its psalm says about being forgiven. Then have each group share its insights with the entire group.

Write the Focus Verse on the board. Give each preteen a foam plate, and set out washable and permanent markers. Have kids write the verse on their plates, using a washable marker to write the first phrase and a permanent marker to write the second one. Ask:

• **What does God do with our sin when we confess?**

Have preteens wash their plates in the bowl and see "God's anger" disappear. Then have them form pairs. Ask partners to tell each other about times God must have been upset with them. Suggest that they use washable markers to write their own sins on the foam plates and rinse "the sins" away. Have partners share the ways that God's favor has remained with them.

POUR OUT YOUR HEART

Help the preteens go through Psalm 30, this awesome testimony to God's grace. Assign one of the following to each pair: verses 1, 2-3, 5b, 7. Give each pair a clean foam plate, and explain that they'll be doing the same thing you did for verse 5a. They'll need to read through their passages and find the negatives and the positive effects of God's love. Have them write the negatives in washable marker and the positives in permanent marker.

Place the bowl of water in the middle of the group. Then have kids take turns around the circle putting the plate into the bowl and then reading the words that remain. Your prayer time should go something like this:

> **O Lord my God,**
> **"I will exalt you, O Lord, for you lifted me out of the depths** [written in permanent marker] **and did not let my enemies gloat over me** [written in washable marker]. **I called to you for help** [washable] **and you healed me** [permanent]." **"You brought me up from the grave** [permanent]; **you spared me from going down into the pit"** [permanent]. **"For his anger lasts only a moment** [washable], **but his favor lasts a lifetime** [permanent]; **weeping may remain for a night** [washable], **but rejoicing comes in the morning"** [permanent].
>
> **"I was dismayed when you hid your face** [washable], **but you made my mountain stand firm** [permanent]." **"You turned my wailing** [washable] **into dancing** [permanent]; **you removed my sackcloth** [washable—explain that wearing sackcloth is a mourning custom] **and clothed me with joy** [permanent—ask preteens to pray with you] **that my heart may sing to you and not be silent. O Lord my God, I will give you thanks forever!"**

Use putty to hang the plates in a row around the room as a reminder of God's favor.

PICKING THE PATH OF HIS PLEASING

Overview: Preteens will choose string "paths" and explore the consequences of their choices.

Focus Verses: "Show me your ways, O Lord, teach me your paths; guide me in your truth and teach me, for you are God my Savior and my hope is in you all day long" (Psalm 25:4-5).

Materials: You'll need Bibles, yarn in two different colors, index cards, tape, scissors, and markers.

Preparation: Set up a maze for this activity by taping one end of a skein of yarn to a chair. Wind the yarn over and around chairs and tables. Cut the yarn off, and tape the cut end to an index card that reads: "Put to shame." Make enough yarn paths with the same color of yarn for each pair of students to have one, and make the paths cross over each other. Have all these paths end with cards that read "Put to shame." Make an extra path with yarn of a different color. Have that path end with a card that has the words of Psalm 25:9 written on it. After you've set up the maze, keep the door closed.

 LIVING PSALM

Have preteens sit in the hall to answer these questions:

- **Have you ever felt confused? Explain.**

- **How can you know the right thing to do?**

- **If you choose the wrong path in life, what can happen to you?**

• EXTRA IMPACT •

Suggest that preteens use a thesaurus to replace words in a psalm to "translate" it into everyday language. Illustrate the activity by writing the Focus Verse on the board, and encourage students to try this activity in their prayer journals.

Show: teach, guide, direct, lead, tell me what way to take, instruct, confide

Me: Carol, your child

Your: Yours, God, and not the world's or my friends'

Ways: paths, truth, will, plans, desires, wishes, dreams, decisions

O Lord: God, My Father, Jesus, King, Savior, Mighty One

Have kids come into the room in pairs. Each pair can select any piece of yarn except for the different-colored one. Partners in each pair will work together to untangle their yarn piece and wind it up. All the pairs will work at the same time. While they're working, have each pair make up a story about a person who made wrong decisions in his or her life without asking God for guidance. Each pair should tell about their person's bad choices and consequences. For example, a pair might make up a story like this one: **Max hated his teacher. He never asked for help with his reading, and he kept falling behind. He paid his older brother to do his homework. Then, in high school, it got tougher to hide the fact that he couldn't read very well. He lied to his parents about his schoolwork and grades. Finally, Max flunked out. He ended up working here and there at odd jobs, never really going anywhere or making anything of himself.**

When pairs have gotten to the cards at the end of the yarn, give everyone a Bible. Ask kids read aloud Psalm 25:4-5 together while you wind up the last piece of yarn (the different-colored piece) into a ball. Read aloud the verse written on the index card at the end. Ask:

- **How will God show us the path of his pleasing?**

- **What do we need to do?**

Assign each pair one of these verses to look up in order to answer this question: Psalm 25:5, 9, 10, 12, and 14. When they've found answers, have them share their answers with the whole group.

Have pairs write the answers on the backs of their index cards and the Focus Verse on the front.

 ## POUR OUT YOUR HEART

Have pairs unroll their yarn pieces, and have the whole class wind all the yarn pieces slowly together while praying Psalm 25:4-5 aloud.

WHIPPED-CREAM PRAYERS

Overview: Preteens will make whipped-cream peaks out of sorrowful puddles to experience waiting on God.

Focus Verse: "How long must I wrestle with my thoughts and every day have sorrow in my heart?" (Psalm 13:2a).

Materials: You'll need Bibles, a cooler with ice, one pint of heavy whipping cream, sugar, an electric mixer, a bowl, a spoon, shortbread or muffins, and napkins.

Preparation: Pack the whipping cream and the mixer blades in the cooler to keep them cold.

 ## LIVING PSALM

Gather kids around the mixer, and ask:

- **Have you ever wanted something really badly? How hard was it to wait?**

- **What are some feelings you have while you're waiting?**

Say: **It's hard to wait. The more you want something, the harder it is to wait. David waited for relief from his enemy, Saul, for about ten years. He had to hide in caves and out in the wilderness, eating off the land and sleeping on rocks. Like us, sometimes David just got tired of waiting.** Pour the whipping cream into the bowl and add two tablespoons of sugar. **Waiting for our pain to pass or our circumstances to change is like being in this puddle of cream.**

Have kids turn to Psalm 13. While they read this psalm aloud together, start the electric mixer on high. Have the group read the psalm aloud over and over again. Ask kids to try to memorize it while the cream whips, which will take about ten minutes. Tell kids that this psalm is a perfect example of David's work. He honestly tells God how he feels and begs God for help, but he always remembers who he is talking to. The psalm ends on a note of rejoicing.

LEADER TIP

The colder the cream and mixing blades are, the faster the cream will become whipped cream. Always start with dry utensils.

When the cream is stiff, use a spoon to form peaks, and say: **God took David's puddles of sorrows and turned them into something sweet. He took his valleys of need and turned them into mountain peaks of joy. God helped David, and he will help you.** Scoop the whipped cream onto shortbread or muffins, and give each person a snack. While kids are eating, ask:

- **What did David do while he was waiting?**

- **What did God do for him?**

- **What can you do as you wait for the Lord?**

Say: **While he was waiting, David took his puddles of sorrows to God in this psalm. You can do this, too.**

• EXTRA IMPACT •

Explain to preteens that God was able to do amazing things through David because David allowed God to work rather than taking matters into his own hands. Have kids look up and read aloud these passages on waiting: Psalm 27:14; 37:7-8; and 37:34. Then have kids form smaller groups to read about David's life in 1 Samuel 18; 19; 24; 26; and 2 Samuel 3; 14. Ask them to note the times David needed to wait for God.

 ## POUR OUT YOUR HEART

Have preteens try to pray Psalm 13 from memory.

TEARS IN A BOTTLE

Overview: Preteens will make "teardrops" and store them in keepsake bottles to help them remember that God treasures their tears.

Focus Verse: "You have seen me tossing and turning through the night. You have collected all my tears and preserved them in your bottle! You have recorded every one in your book" (Psalm 56:8; The Living Bible).

Materials: You'll need Bibles; newsprint, tape, and a marker or a dry-erase board and marker; water; salt; vegetable oil; small bowl; spoon; adhesive labels; pens; and an empty jar or bottle for each preteen.

Preparation: None is needed.

> **• EXTRA IMPACT •**
>
> Explain to preteens that getting the grief out is the first step in healing a broken heart. Then ask them to look up these passages in 2 Samuel to discover other ways the Israelites expressed their sorrows: 1:11-12, 17; 3:31-36; 12:16-17; 13:19, 30-31; and 15:30.

 LIVING PSALM

Ask:

- **Do any of you collect anything? What? Why?**

Say: **God collects something dear to him.** Write the words of the Focus Verse, Psalm 56:8, on a dry-erase board or newsprint.

Say: **Every teardrop that rolls down your cheek, and all the tears inside you that won't come out, are treasured in the heart of your God who loves you. Sometimes, in olden days in the East, the people at funerals would catch their tears in bottles and place them at the tombs of their loved ones. Not a single teardrop or sad sigh goes unnoticed by your heavenly Father.**

Give each preteen an empty jar or bottle, and ask a few volunteers to mix water, salt, and a little oil in a bowl. When the "teardrops" have been mixed, have each person pour some of the mixture in his or her jar or bottle. Then give each person an adhesive label and a pen. Tell kids that they can write on the labels either the Focus Verse or this rhyme: "Somewhere in my Father's keeping is a bottle of my weeping."

While kids work, say: **Besides cleaning our eyes, tears help to wash away the sorrow in our soul. Haven't you felt better after a good cry? Actually, a special hormone is released when we cry, and this hormone makes us feel better. God gave us tears. Jesus shed real tears. David wept aloud until his strength was gone. Don't be ashamed of your tears. They are God-made, God-given, and treasured by God.**

Have kids form pairs, and ask pairs to discuss each of these questions. Explain that, if a question is too personal, kids can choose to pass or to write a response. Ask:

- **What feelings bring on your tears?**
- **When was the last time you cried?**
- **If you could, what would you cry about?**

 POUR OUT YOUR HEART

Have each person in the class wipe a small "teardrop" under one eye. Have kids take turns filling in the blank as you pray this prayer. The "tears" will be dried at the end of the prayer.

Dear Lord:
You have seen me tossing and turning through the night. You have collected all my tears and preserved them in your bottle! I have been sad about _____.
You have recorded every one of my tears in your book. Thank you for caring so much. Thank you for loving me so much. Amen.

HE SETS THE LONELY IN FAMILIES

Overview: Preteens will record praises for each other.

Focus Verse: "God sets the lonely in families" (Psalm 68:6a).

Materials: You'll need Bibles, paper, and pens.

Preparation: None is needed.

> **• EXTRA IMPACT •**
> Think about making these papers into special keepsakes by using bordered paper. People who have participated in this type of exercise have been known to keep these papers with them for many years. Don't forget to include your name on a piece of paper—you deserve this "upper" too!

LIVING PSALM

Say: **Have you ever felt lonely even with a lot of people around you? Sometimes you can be lonely and not even realize it. You can be doing what you want to do and be surrounded by people and still be lonely for a special friend. We all need a special friend to share good times and bad times with. We need someone we care about who cares about us.**

Have preteens form pairs to answer these questions:

- **When do you feel lonely?**

- **Who do you feel loneliest around?**

- **Who helps you to not feel lonely?**

Say: **God understands our tendency to hide inside ourselves, so he came up with an answer. He puts us in the family of God.** Give each person a Bible, and ask kids to read Psalm 68:6 aloud together. Say: **When you become a Christian, you become part of a worldwide family. Every Christian is your brother or sister. As Christians, it's our job to be family to one another by affirming each other.**

Hand each preteen a piece of paper and a pen. Ask each person to write his or her first name across the top of the paper in large letters. Then ask kids to hand the paper to the person on the left. As kids receive the papers, ask them to write one positive comment about the person whose name is on the paper and then pass the papers to the left again. Tell them that they don't need to sign their names to the comments.

Every preteen should write something positive about everyone else in the group. The only rule is that comments should not be about physical appearance, clothes, status, or possessions. Instead, comments should be uplifting statements about character qualities. For example, a paper might have these comments on it: "You always make me laugh," "I am touched by your prayers," and "You are so thoughtful."

POUR OUT YOUR HEART

Write "God" at the top of a piece of paper, and pass it around. Ask each preteen to record a comment to God. Read the paper aloud as a closing prayer.

THE FEELING HAPPY PSALMS

STOP, ASK, GO

Overview: Preteens will go through a maze, stopping at each turn to ask for God's advice.

Focus Verse: "I will instruct you and teach you in the way you should go; I will counsel you and watch over you" (Psalm 32:8).

Materials: You'll need Bibles, masking tape, dice, paper and pens.

Preparation: Use masking tape to outline a maze on the floor. Include multiple intersections and several possible exits.

LIVING PSALM

Say: **One of God's most precious promises is that he will instruct us in the way we should go.** Give each preteen a Bible, and have kids read Psalm 32:8 aloud together. Say: **Even David got confused at times. When he was confused, he asked God for clear direction before taking a step. In the two books of Samuel, which record David's life, we can see David asking God for direction.**

David and the priest had an unusual way of getting God's answer. David would inquire or ask of the Lord through the priest. The priest would ask God for his answer by taking the Urim and the Thummim from the special vest he wore, which was called an ephod. The Urim and Thummim were one way to find God's will for the Israelite nation. No one really knows exactly what they were or how they worked. They could have been jewels that glowed the right answer, or they could have been like dice that revealed God's response. We do know that, when David stopped and asked for God's advice, things went well for him. When he forged ahead, forgetting to stop and ask God for direction, disaster followed.

Designate a starting point in the maze, and have preteens take turns going through it. Players should walk to an intersection, stop there, and roll the dice. If the number is odd, the player should turn left. If the number is even, the player should turn right. When the player gets to an exit, he or she can sit down at that spot until everyone gets through the maze. Ask:

- **Did everyone end up in the same spot? How is that like our walk with God?**

- **Psalm 32:9 says "Do not be like the horse or the mule, which have no understanding but must be controlled by bit and bridle or they will not come to you." What does this verse tell you about the conditions God places on his promise of teaching us?**

- **When in your life should you stop and ask God for his direction?**

- **How does God answer our requests for guidance today?**

> ### • EXTRA IMPACT •
> Explain to the preteens that, while we don't have the Urim and Thummim today, we do have the Bible to help us discern God's will. In addition, God speaks to us through the Holy Spirit in prayer, in our circumstances, and in God's people when we're confused. Have kids write down the Focus Verse and these four ways we can discern God's will.

 ## POUR OUT YOUR HEART

Give preteens paper and pens, and have them work together to create a personalized version of Psalm 32:8-9. Then have them pray their psalm together. Here's a sample:

Dear Lord:
Thank you for promising to teach me about the way that I should go. Please counsel me and watch over me. Help me to not be like a stubborn horse but to follow your will for my life. Amen.

THE HEART OF GOD IN THE HEART OF GOD'S WORD

Overview: Preteens will make their own acrostic from Psalm 119 and share it with a younger class.

Focus Verse: "Your statutes are my heritage forever; they are the joy of my heart" (Psalm 119:111).

Materials: You'll need Bibles, paper, pens, and paper clips.

Preparation: None is needed.

LIVING PSALM

Say: **If you ever feel uncertain about life, you can go to God's Word. And in the Bible is a special psalm written about the Word of God.** Give each person a Bible, and have kids turn to Psalm 119 and thumb through it. Ask them what they notice.

Say: **This Psalm was written with a lot of care. It is an acrostic. It has twenty-two stanzas, one for each letter of the Hebrew alphabet. You can see the Hebrew letter above the stanza. Each stanza has eight verses, and, in the original Hebrew, each verse in a stanza starts with the same letter. We're going to make an alphabetical acrostic out of this special psalm.**

Have preteens form pairs, and give each pair paper and pens. Divide the twenty-six letters of the alphabet evenly between the pairs. Have pairs draw large, fancy letters down the side of their paper. Then have pairs look up verses in Psalm 119 that could fit with each letter of the acrostic. Have them write the verses in their own words. Here's a sample:

A—Always obey God's laws, forever and ever (verse 44).

B—By living according to your Word, I will keep my way pure (verse 9).

C—Choose the way of truth. Set your heart on God's laws (verse 30).

Ask a volunteer to design a children's book cover, using the Focus Verse as the title. When pairs are finished with their acrostics, gather the pages, and make copies of each page for every person in the group. Then make copies for a kindergarten or first-grade class in your church. Let the kids assemble the pages into books. They can read their books aloud to younger kids, who can color in the fat letters and take the books home. After the project, ask:

- **What are some benefits of living according to God's Word?**

- **How can you keep God's Word in your heart?**

- **What do you love about God's Word?**

Say: **God gave us his Word to guide us and teach us how to live for him. It's important to spend some time daily reading God's Word, even if only for a few minutes. God's Word is our life and breath!**

 ## Pour out Your Heart

Notice that the writer of this psalm goes back and forth between talking to the reader and talking to God. Many of the psalms do this. It's as if God is in the same room with the believers the psalmist is talking to; the psalmist's joy in God's Word bubbles over from God onto the people. Have each preteen choose a prayer verse from Psalm 119, then have them take turns praying their verses.

From Bitter to Sweet: The Psalms of Hope

Overview: Preteens will listen to a psalm about despair turning into hope as they taste bitter and sweet, then they'll think of imagery they can use to present the negative to positive theme.

Focus Verses: "Hear my cry for mercy. My heart leaps for joy and I will give thanks to him in song" (Psalm 28: 2a, 7b).

Materials: You'll need Bibles; unsweetened cocoa, chocolate, napkins, and copies of the "From Bitter to Sweet" margin box (p. 70).

Preparation: Set out the cocoa and chocolate.

Living Psalm

Say: **No matter how bad David's situation was, he never forgot that God was in control. He started so many of his psalms telling God his feelings of woe. And that's a great start. That's what God wants you to do.**

Read Psalm 28:1-5 aloud, and have preteens taste the cocoa while you read.

Say: **But David doesn't stay there, looking inward and feeling sorry for himself. He looks to God. He lets God turn his despair into hope, his bitterness to sweetness.**

Have kids enjoy the chocolate while you read Psalm 28:6-9 aloud. Ask:

- **How is the taste of the cocoa like David's feeling in these verses?**

- **How can this psalm help you look to God when you face problems?**

FROM BITTER TO SWEET

Choose one of these psalms, or find another one you like: Psalms 3; 5; 6; 13; 18; 30; 31; 42; 52; 54–57; 59-61; 63; 64; 70–71; 73; 102; 124; and 140.

Check out the following presentation ideas to get your creative "juices" flowing.

- Dark to light: light candles and blow them out
- Deflated to inflated: blow up balloons
- Alone to together: come together as a group
- Low notes to high notes: play notes on an instrument or sing notes
- Broken to fixed: put together a puzzle or a building toy
- Lost to found: blindfold one member
- Dirty to clean: wash out a stain
- Losing to winning: play a basketball game

Say: **The bitter cocoa is needed to make sweet chocolate. Bitter experiences can help us grow. We may feel bitter when we face hard times, but if we trust God, he will help us learn from the situation. Like David, we can have hope.**

• EXTRA IMPACT •

Ask preteens to compare Psalm 86, which was written by David, to Psalm 88, which was written by the Sons of Korah. What notes do these two psalms end on? Why? What's the missing ingredient in Psalm 88?

Have preteens form pairs. Give each pair a "From Bitter to Sweet" margin box, and ask partners to use the information to help them brainstorm about a unique way to present a psalm that goes from negative to positive. Tell kids that they can either actually do whatever they come up with or just talk about it. When each pair has chosen a psalm and a way to present it, have partners share their psalms and presentations with the whole group.

POUR OUT YOUR HEART

As you pray this prayer, start out hunched over and then slowly stretch to standing as the prayer turns from negative to positive.

Dear Lord:
When we feel sad, lonely, stressed out, afraid, desperate, and angry, we will tell you. We will be honest with you and others about our feelings. But we will remember that you are in control and will help us. We will give thanks to you in song! You are our strength and our shield! Amen.

A LIGHT THAT WON'T GO OUT

Overview: Light a trick candle on a cupcake to see how God keeps our lamps burning.

Focus Verse: "You, O Lord, keep my lamp burning; my God turns my darkness into light" (Psalm 18:28).

Materials: You'll need Bibles, supplies to bake cupcakes, a red gumdrop, a bowl of water, relighting candles, regular candles, matches, napkins, a knife, a foam plate, and a marker.

Preparation: Bake cupcakes so that you have one for each person in the group plus at least one extra. As you prepare the cupcakes, put a red gumdrop in the center of one of them, and be sure you know which one has the gumdrop. Put a regular candle on each regular cupcake, and put a relighting candle on the cupcake with the gumdrop.

LIVING PSALM

Give every preteen (except one) a cupcake with a regular candle on it. Give the special cupcake to someone in the group who could use an extra sparkle in his or her day. Ask each preteen to give the cupcake his or her own name and then tell a story about himself or herself in the third person. Ask kids to first say something good that happened to the cupcake "kid." For example, someone might say, "Willie got the video game he'd been wanting for a whole year," or "Daryl was one of only five kids in her school to earn the President's Award." As each person shares, light his or her candle.

Then have preteens tell something negative that happened to their "cupcake kids" and blow out their own candles. For example, one preteen might say, "Willie took his video game to his cousin's house in another state and left it there," or "Even though Daryl worked hard the next year, she didn't win the President's Award."

One preteen won't be able to blow out the candle. Ask:

- **Why won't [person's name]'s candle go out?**

LEADER TIP
Follow the safety instructions with the relighting candles. You may need to extinguish them in water.

Say: **[Person's name]'s candle wouldn't go out to show that you can't put out the light of God.** Cut open the cupcake to show that it's what's inside that makes the difference. Give each preteen a Bible, and have the group read Psalm 18:28. Let kids enjoy the cupcakes while you ask:

• EXTRA IMPACT •
Give each preteen a candle to glue to a piece of black paper. Kids can write the Focus Verse under the candle in bright colors and add glow-in-the-dark fabric paint as rays shining forth from the candle. Turn the lights off to see how God keeps our light shining!

- **Why is it that you can't extinguish joy in a believer?**

- **Does that mean we'll always feel wonderful? Why or why not?**

 ## POUR OUT YOUR HEART

Write the Focus Verse on the foam plate. Put a cupcake with a relighting candle on the plate. Light the candle, and then pass it around, giving each person a chance to pray the verse to God and try to blow out the candle.

> **Dear God:**
> **You, O Lord, keep my lamp burning; my God, you turn my darkness into light! Amen.**

PRAISE GOD IN THE ASSEMBLY

Overview: Preteens will stand up and repeat a psalm in the church service to thank the God they love.

Focus Verse: "I will give you thanks in the great assembly; among throngs of people I will praise you" (Psalm 35:18).

Materials: You'll need Bibles, index cards, and pens.

Preparation: Check with your pastor before planning this devotion for the church service. Find a praise song, preferably one that uses some of the psalms, that you can lead after the preteens' testimony.

 ## LIVING PSALM

Say: **God's book, the Bible, is an open love letter to us. God shouts aloud from each page, "I love you. I love you. You are my precious treasure, my own adored children!" God is proud of us. Are we proud of him? Have you ever told anyone how much you love God? Now is your chance.**

Read the Focus Verse, Psalm 35:18, aloud, and say: **You're going to have the chance to thank God "in the great assembly."** Give each person a Bible, an index card, and a pen. Ask kids to read through some psalms of praise, such as Psalms 24; 93; 95-101; 103; 134; 136; and 145-150, and choose their favorite verses. Ask each person to practice saying his or her chosen verse aloud several times. Then ask each preteen to write on the index card one thing he or she is thankful to God for and would like to share in the church service.

When kids have finished, help them decide the order in which they'll share, and have each person practice standing up, reading his or her verse aloud, thanking God aloud, and then sitting down.

In the sanctuary or worship area, have preteens sit in various places throughout the church, preferably with their families. At the designated time in the service, have the preteens share in the order that was decided earlier. After they're finished, ask if anyone else would like to stand up to give thanks to God. Then lead the entire congregation in singing the praise song to God.

• EXTRA IMPACT •

Psalm 148 is another psalm of pure praise. Let preteens choose a conductor and their own "instruments" to praise God using this psalm. Have kids each draw a picture of the "heaven," "great sea creatures," and other images in this psalm. Then have the conductor lead them in standing with their pictures at the appropriate time.

When you've returned to the room, ask:

- **How did it feel to give God "thanks in the great assembly"?**

- **Why is it important to praise God "among throngs of people"?**

- **What stops you from acknowledging God around friends who are nonbelievers?**

- **How can you praise God around your friends who are nonbelievers?**

Say: **David honored God publicly. God honored David back publicly. David loved God and even risked looking like a fanatic by dancing for God with all his might. Singing his thoughts aloud, David led his whole nation in worship. We may not be able to do that, but we *can* worship God in our daily lives.**

 ## POUR OUT YOUR HEART

Use Psalm 136 in a "concert" of thanksgiving. Have the girls read the praise lines and the boys repeat the refrain, "His love endures forever."

PSALM 151—MY OWN SONG

Overview: Preteens will discover how to make Scripture personally meaningful by writing their own psalms of praise to God.

Focus Verse: "The Lord is my rock, my fortress and my deliverer; my God is my rock, in whom I take refuge. He is my shield and the horn of my salvation, my stronghold" (Psalm 18:2).

Materials: You'll need Bibles, paper, pens, and copies of "My Own Psalm" (p. 75).

Preparation: None is needed.

 ## LIVING PSALM

Give each person a Bible, and ask preteens to read Psalm 18:2 aloud together. Ask:

- **What is God to David, according to this Psalm?**

- **Why would David describe God as a fortress, a shield, and a stronghold?**

- **Can you relate to this? Why or why not?**

> ## • EXTRA IMPACT •
> Can any of your preteens put their psalms to music? Encourage musical kids to write down their favorite descriptions of God, and ask them to try their hand at composition at home.

Say: **David was a warrior. He killed a lot of soldiers in battle, and he had a lot of enemies constantly after him. In one of the psalms, David said those who hated him outnumbered the hairs on his head. But God protected, sheltered, and defended him. As a soldier, David used words connected with war to describe God's protection. But fortresses and strongholds are just not something that many people can personally relate to if they've never been in a battle.**

But a soccer player might think of God as the coach who guides him, the goal he aims for, or the trophy to capture. An artist might think of God as a model and a palette full of colors. Ask:

- **How might a baby think of God?**

Ask kids to think about imagery that connects with their own lives. Then ask them to think about how they could use that imagery to describe what God means to them. Give each person a copy of "My Own Psalm" and a pen, and ask kids to write a psalm using their imagery.

 ## POUR OUT YOUR HEART

Have each person read one line from his or her own psalm. Continue in this manner until preteens have read all of their work.

DANCING IN THE DARK

Overview: Preteens will develop a pantomime production to celebrate the deeds of our active God.

Focus Verses: "Give thanks to the Lord, call on his name; make known among the nations what he has done. Sing to him, sing praise to him; tell of all his wonderful acts" (Psalm 105:1-2).

Materials: You'll need Bibles, a pair of thin white gloves for each person (available in photographic-supply stores), and a black light (available in hardware stores or party-supply stores).

Preparation: Before this meeting, ask preteens to come dressed in dark, long-sleeved shirts and dark pants, but don't tell them why. Invite another class to see your "production."

LIVING PSALM

Say: **Our God isn't asleep or lazy. We serve an incredible, dynamic, living, active God! His ears are alert, and he's ready to leap to your defense or wipe away your tears. Psalm 105 recites God's hand in Israel's history.**

Give each person a Bible, and have preteens turn to Psalm 105. Read it aloud, and ask the kids to listen for all the action words in this psalm. Then ask a volunteer reader to read through the psalm again and pause at each action word. Have kids think of hand motions to demonstrate God's actions in this psalm. For example, for verse 5, which says, "Remember the wonders he has done," the hand motion could be extending fingers one at a time as it counting. Have preteens practice their motions as you read the psalm. Then give each preteen a pair of gloves. Turn on the black light, and have kids line up and dramatize the psalm together as you read it aloud. After you've practiced several times, invite another group to see your production. After the drama is over, ask:

> ## LEADER TIP
> White cotton seems to reflect the black light better than polyester. Also, you can purchase a black light less expensively at a hardware store but more completely assembled at a party-supply store. You may also be able to rent or borrow a black light. Call around for prices and information first.

- **How can knowing what God did for his people in the past make a difference in your life today?**

- **What can God do?**

- **What can God do for you?**

Say: **God doesn't change. He is the same active, living God today that he was in the past. He still performs miracles for his people.** Talk about some miracles God has done in our recent history and in kids' own lives.

MY OWN PSALM

O Lord, for me...

you are the friend who shares secrets with me.

you are the sibling who is always there for me.

you are the parent who protects me.

you are the teacher who teaches me.

you are the doctor who heals me.

you are the leader who encourages me.

you are the crowd that claps for me.

you are the food that fills me.

you are the mystery that puzzles me.

you are the map that directs me.

you are the rainbow that shines over me.

you are the colors that brighten me.

you are the wisdom that whispers to me.

you are the hand that stops me.

you are the foot that moves me.

you are the smile that won't leave me.

you are the discovery that delights me.

you are the eyes that see through me.

you are the shadow that follows me.

you are the wonder that wanders through me.

you are the sculptor who shapes me.

I love you. I need you. Amen.

O Lord, for me...

_____

_____

_____

_____

_____

_____

_____

_____

_____

_____

_____

_____

_____

_____

_____

_____

_____

_____

_____

_____

_____

I love you. I need you. Amen.

Let each preteen keep his or her pair of gloves. Kids can place them in their prayer journals and wear them when they pray to God with an earnest need for God to act on their behalf.

POUR OUT YOUR HEART

Have the preteens pray their way through this psalm together, starting with verse 8. Ask them to watch for the action words they identified, and ask them to use the present tense for those action words as they come to them. For example, kids would say, "You remember" or "You command."

> **• EXTRA IMPACT •**
> Invite someone who "speaks" sign language to your class. Ask your guest to sign this psalm using gloves and the black light.

A PSALM MY SIZE

Overview: Preteens will memorize a favorite verse as they write it into the shape of their names.

Focus Verse: "Surely God is my help; the Lord is the one who sustains me" (Psalm 54:4).

Materials: You'll need Bibles; newsprint, tape, and a marker or a dry erase board and marker; paper; markers; pens; and a copy of "My Favorite Psalms" for each preteen (p. 78).

Preparation: List these references on the newsprint or dry erase board: Psalms 9:10; 13:6; 16:8; 27:1; 27:14; 37:4; 55:22; 56:9; 103:11; and 107:9.

LIVING PSALM

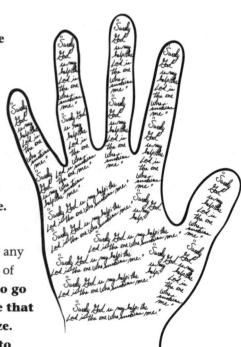

Say: **The neat thing about the Psalms is that we can all find ourselves in them. They speak our language. They speak about our feelings, our hopes, our fears, and our dreams. When David and the other authors wrote the Psalms, they rarely gave specific information about their own personal situations. That's why each psalm is like a warm comforter for any weary traveler . Everyone needs a favorite verse from the Psalms that's just his or her size. I've listed some special ones on the board.**

Encourage preteens to look up the verses and note any that they especially like. Give each person two pieces of paper, a black marker, and a pen. Say: **I'd like you to go through the Psalms and find one special verse that you would like to memorize. Then use a black marker to trace your hand on one page. Lay the second piece of white paper on top of the first. Write your favorite psalm over and over in tiny letters to fill in the shape of your hand. When you lift up the top paper, you'll have God's word shaped into you!**

> **LEADER TIP**
> Don't forget to join the kids in their journey of discovery. These activities work for adults too!

• EXTRA IMPACT •

Make "My Favorite Psalms" books to give away as gifts. Kids can color the borders, fill pages of verses, and make a cover out of heavier paper. These can be used to encourage people going through hard times. Kids might make books for themselves; they could even reduce the book to pocket-size to put in their school backpacks for a lift from God during the school day.

Have each person share his or her verse with the group. Then give everyone a "My Favorite Psalms" handout. Tell kids they can start working on the sheet in class and then take it home to put in their prayer journals. Have them copy down any favorite passages and then describe how each passage makes them feel. Ask:

- **What verse did you choose as your favorite? Why did you choose it?**

- **What feeling do you get from that verse?**

- **How can it be helpful to copy your favorite verses?**

 POUR OUT YOUR HEART

Have each preteen pray his or her favorite verse to God.

QUALITIES TO LIVE BY

Overview: Preteens will identify special qualities God gave them and consider how God may use those qualities in their lives.

Focus Verse: "I praise you because I am fearfully and wonderfully made" (Psalm 139:14a).

Materials: You'll need Bibles, pens, and copies of the "Wonderfully Me; Wonderful Life" handout (p. 80).

Preparation: None is needed.

 LIVING PSALM

Give each preteen a pen and a copy of "Wonderfully Me; Wonderful Life."

Say: **Every one of us is unique. We all look different from each other, we talk differently from one another, and we have different and special qualities. Take a few minutes to think about the qualities you have. Then list those qualities on your handout.**

After kids have had a few minutes to list qualities, ask:

- **What it easy or hard to make your list of qualities? Explain.**

- **What is the special quality you are most pleased with?**

Have volunteers read a verse each of Psalm 139:13-16.

Say: **This psalm talks about God creating us as wonderful beings. And verse 16 tells us God knows all about our lives—even the parts of our lives that haven't happened yet!**

Now's your chance to dream a little. Look at the qualities you listed. Then think about how God might use those qualities in your life.

Point out the "My Life" column in the handout. Have kids choose some of the qualities they

MY FAVORITE PSALMS

My Favorite Verses From Psalms	This Verse Makes Me Feel...

listed in the first column and use the second column to describe ways God might use those qualities. After a few minutes, ask:

- **What was it like thinking about your future?**

- **How has this activity helped you appreciate your God-given qualities more?**

 ## POUR OUT YOUR HEART

This entire psalm is a prayer of praise. Have each person pick out a favorite verse from this psalm and put it into his or her own words. For example:

O Lord:

It was you who created me as I am, inside and out. You wove me together inside my mother before I was born. I praise and thank you because of the awesome way that you made me. I look forward to the life you've given me. Thank you. Amen.

• EXTRA IMPACT •

Encourage kids to practice sharing their God-given gifts. If a preteen wrote that he or she is good at reading, encourage that preteen to read to a younger child this week. Next time you meet, have kids share how they made life better for someone else.

Wonderfully Me; Wonderful Life

My Qualities

Think about the qualities you were created with. You have special qualities that no one else has. List them below:

_____

_____

_____

_____

_____

_____

_____

_____

_____

_____

My Life

Think about the qualities you listed. Choose several of these qualities, then describe next to each how you think God might use that quality in your life.

_____

_____

_____

_____

_____

_____

_____

_____

_____

_____

Dear Parent(s),

Your child is learning to recognize his or her own feelings and turn those feeling over to the Lord, as David did in the Psalms. Listed here are questions you can use as a way of bonding with your child and to help your preteen explore his or her own treasure chest of emotions.

Icebreakers

- What color do you think a mad polar would be?
- If you had six arms, what could you do better?
- If you could choose anyone to be a Siamese twin with you, who would you choose?
- If you could make an ice-cream pizza, what would it taste like?
- If you could be a mouse in someone's house, whose house would it be?
- Imagine that you're a world-famous sculptor. Your finest work is about to be seen for the first time. It's a _____.

Sharing Feelings

- When was the last time you felt [name a feeling]?
- How do you feel about [name a person]?
- What would you like to do when you feel [name a feeling]?
- What would you like *me* to do when you feel [name a feeling]?
- What emotions do you feel at [name a place]? When?
- What is you favorite feeling? Why?
- What can I do to help you share your feelings?
- How would you prefer to share your feelings—by telling someone, writing about your feeling in a prayer journal, drawing a prayer, singing a song, or something else?
- When is the best time to talk? When is the worst time?
- If you could let yourself really cry about something, what would you cry about?
- What would you like to talk to me about that we never seem to talk about?
- What question would you most like to ask me?
- What question would you most like me to ask you?
- What stops you from talking to me?
- When you have a problem, what do you usually want from me—sympathy (feeling sorry for you) or a solution?

God bless you and your child.

Sincerely,

Scripture Index

Topic Index

Group Publishing, Inc.
Attention: Product Development
P.O. Box 481
Loveland, CO 80539
Fax: (970) 679-4370

Evaluation for
Emotion Explosion! 40 Devotions for Preteen Ministry

Please help Group Publishing, Inc. continue to provide innovative and useful resources for ministry. Please take a moment to fill out this evaluation and mail or fax it to us. Thanks!

● ● ●

1. As a whole, this book has been (circle one)

not very helpful   very helpful

1   2   3   4   5   6   7   8   9   10

2. The best things about this book:

3. Ways this book could be improved:

4. Things I will change because of this book:

5. Other books I'd like to see Group publish in the future:

6. Would you be interested in field-testing future Group products and giving us your feedback? If so, please fill in the information below:

Name _____

Church Name _____

Denomination _____ Church Size _____

Church Address _____

City _____ State _____ ZIP _____

Church Phone _____

E-mail _____

More Resources for Your Preteen Ministry!

Dynamic Preteen Ministry

Gordon West & Becki West

This essential guide to building a "no-miss" preteen ministry will help you minister to preteens as they make the difficult transition from childhood to adolescence. The authors offer solid, practical and comprehensive understanding on how to build an effective, real-life ministry to reach this vital age group. Both children's and youth workers will better understand the mind and emotions of 10- to 14-year olds, "bridge the gap" between children's ministry and youth ministry, and strengthen existing programs with recommended activities.

ISBN 0-7644-2084-4

No-Miss Lessons for Preteen Kids

Let's just come out and say it: 5th- and 6th-graders can be a tough crowd. Sweet as sugar one week and sweet as sugar in your gas tank the next, getting their attention can be a challenge. Fortunately, it's a challenge you're ready to meet with these 22 faith-building, active-learning lessons that deal with self-esteem…relationships…making choices…and other topics. Perfect for Sunday school, meeting groups, or weekend retreats and (are you sure about this?) lock-ins!

ISBN 0-7644-2015-1

Smart Choices for Preteen Kids

Help your kids make good decisions with these 20 faith-building lessons. Plus, these relational lessons help kids form a solid, Christian support group—friends to encourage them during tough times. Your preteens will apply what they learn…and be better prepared to confront their teenage years. This book is a must for Sunday school teachers and leaders of 5th- and 6th-grade groups.

ISBN 0-7644-2039-9

More Smart Choices for Preteen Kids

Want kids to make good choices about their faith? Their friends? The world? Then share these 20 faith-building lessons with your preteenagers. Children's leaders will pass along the Bible truths kids need to make smart choices, and help kids form solid, supportive Christian friendships. Includes 20 complete meetings, including commitment sections that take kids deep into Bible truths.

ISBN 0-7644-2110-7

Exciting Resources for Your Children's Ministry

Sunday School Specials Series

Lois Keffer

This best-selling series is a lifesaver for small churches that combine age groups...large churches that host family nights...and small groups with kids to entertain. Each book provides an entire quarter of active-learning experiences, interactive Bible stories, life applications, and take-home handouts. Children love them because they're fun and you'll love the easy preparation!

Sunday School Specials	ISBN 1-55945-082-7
Sunday School Specials 2	ISBN 1-55945-177-7
Sunday School Specials 3	ISBN 1-55945-606-X
Sunday School Specials 4	ISBN 0-7644-2050-X

The Children's Worker's Encyclopedia of Bible-Teaching Ideas

You get over 350 attention-grabbing, active-learning devotions...art and craft projects...creative prayers...service projects...field trips...music suggestions...quiet reflection activities...skits...and more—winning ideas from each and every book of the Bible! Simple, step-by-step directions and handy indexes make it easy to slide an idea into any meeting—on short notice—with little or no preparation!

Old Testament	ISBN 1-55945-622-1
New Testament	ISBN 1-55945-625-6

5-Minute Messages for Children

Donald Hinchey

It's easy to share meaningful messages that your children will enjoy and remember! Here are 52 short, Bible-based messages for you to use in Sunday school, children's church, or midweek meetings.

	ISBN 1-55945-030-4
5-Minute Messages and More	ISBN 0-7644-2038-0

Just-Add-Kids Games for Children's Ministry

If your classroom is stocked with the basics (chairs, paper, a light switch and masking tape) then you've got everything you need to play dozens of great new games! You get high-energy games...low-energy games...and everything in between. Some games have Bible applications, some require no supplies at all, and every game takes just moments to explain.

ISBN 0-7644-2112-3

More Resources for Your Children's Ministry

Quick Children's Sermons 2: Why Did God Make Mosquitoes?

Now you're ready to answer some of the most common questions kids ask about God...Jesus...heaven...and life as they observe it. You get 50 more befuddling questions straight from the lips of God's smallest saints...and great answers, too! Use this warm, witty book as a year's supply of children's sermons...for Sunday school...or to launch discussions in class or children's church!

ISBN 0-7644-2052-6

Crazy Clothesline Characters

Carol Mader

You're already familiar with these Bible stories—The Creation, Noah's Ark, Nebuchadnezzar, Jonah, Jesus' Birth, The Prodigal Son and 34 others. But now you have 40 new and fun ways to tell them to your children! You'll tell stories with cue cards, food, walks, flashlights, balloons and other multi-sensory items to involve children in the story...and to help them remember it for a lifetime!

ISBN 0-7644-2140-9

The Ultimate Bible Guide for Children's Ministry

You want your kids to know the difference between the Old and New Testaments. To quickly and easily find Bible verses. To understand the Bible and be comfortable exploring God's Word. Start here! These kid-friendly, 5- to 15-minute activities help children from preschool through 6th grade master the skills that make Bible reading fun. Give kids a rock-solid foundation for using the Bible—and do it without boring kids.

ISBN 0-7644-2076-3

Amazing Science Devotions for Children's Ministry

Kids love figuring out how stuff works, so put their natural curiosity to work! From "What makes popcorn pop?" to "Where do rainbows come from?" here's tons of science fun that connects kids with God's wonderful world. For children's sermons...Sunday school...midweek programs and clubs...anywhere you want to give kids' faith a boost and help them learn about God!

ISBN 0-7644-2105-0